'NOH'

OR

ACCOMPLISHMENT

A Study of the Classical Stage of Japan

BY
ERNEST FENOLLOSA
AND
EZRA POUND

PELICAN PUBLISHING COMPANY
Gretna 1999

Copyright © 1916
By Ernest Fenollosa and Ezra Pound

First edition published by Macmillan, 1916
Second edition published by Alfred A. Knopf, 1917
First Pelican edition, 1999

Library of Congress Cataloging-in-Publication Data

Fenollosa, Ernest Francisco, 1853-1908.
    'Noh' or Accomplishment : a study of the classical stage of
Japan / by Ernest Fenollosa and Ezra Pound.
      p.   cm.
    Originally published: London : Macmillan, 1916.
    Includes texts of several plays, translated from Japanese by Ezra
Pound.
    ISBN 1-56554-440-4 (alk. paper)
    1. No. 2. No plays—Translations into English.   I. Pound, Ezra,
1885-1972. II. Title: 'Noh'. III. Title: Accomplishment.
PN2924.5.N6F46 1999
792'.0952—dc21   98-55492
                                                                      CIP

*Some of the plays and part of the notes in this book have previously appeared
in "Poetry," "Drama," "The Quarterly Review," "The Quarterly Note-Book,"
and "Certain Noble Plays of Japan."*

Printed in India   #40559764

Published by Pelican Publishing Company, Inc.
1000 Burmaster Street, Gretna, Louisiana 70053

CONTENTS

PART I

PART II

'NOH'

PART III

PART IV

NOTE

THE vision and the plan are Fenollosa's. In the prose I have had but the part of literary executor; in the plays my work has been that of translator who has found all the heavy work done for him and who has had but the pleasure of arranging beauty into the words.

I wish to express my very deep thanks to Mr. Arthur Waley, who has corrected a number of mistakes in the orthography of proper names from such Japanese texts as were available, and who has assisted me out of various impasses where my own ignorance would have left me.

EZRA POUND

PART I

INTRODUCTION

THE life of Ernest Fenollosa was the romance
par excellence of modern scholarship. He went
to Japan as a professor of economics. He
ended as Imperial Commissioner of Arts. He
had unearthed treasure that no Japanese had
heard of. It may be an exaggeration to say
that he had saved Japanese art for Japan, but
it is certain that he had done as much as any
one man could have to set the native art in its
rightful pre-eminence and to stop the apeing
of Europe. He had endeared himself to the
government and laid the basis for a personal
tradition. When he died suddenly in England
the Japanese government sent a warship for
his body, and the priests buried him within
the sacred enclosure at Miidera. These facts
speak for themselves.

His present reputation in Europe rests upon
his " Epochs of Chinese and Japanese Art."
In America he is known also for his service to
divers museums. His work on Japanese and

3

Chinese literature has come as a surprise to the scholars. It forms, I think, the basis for a new donation, for a new understanding of "the East." For instance, as I look over that section of his papers which deals with the Japanese Noh, having read what others have written in English about these plays, I am in a position to say definitely that Professor Fenollosa knew, more of the subject than any one who has yet written in our tongue.

The Noh is unquestionably one of the great arts of the world, and it is quite possibly one of the most recondite.

In the eighth century of our era the dilettante of the Japanese court established the tea cult and the play of "listening to incense." [1]

In the fourteenth century the priests and the court and the players all together produced a drama scarcely less subtle.

For "listening to incense" the company was divided into two parties, and some arbiter burnt many kinds and many blended sorts of perfume, and the game was not merely to know which was which, but to give to each one of them a beautiful and allusive name, to recall by the title some strange event of history or some passage of romance or legend. It was

---

[1] Vide Brinkley, Oriental Series, vol. iii.

a refinement in barbarous times, comparable to the art of polyphonic rhyme, developed in feudal Provence four centuries later, and now almost wholly forgotten.

The art of allusion, or this love of allusion in art, is at the root of the Noh. These plays, or eclogues, were made only for the few ; for the nobles ; for those trained to catch the allusion. In the Noh we find an art built upon the god-dance, or upon some local legend of spiritual apparition, or, later, on gestes of war and feats of history ; an art of splendid posture, of dancing and chanting, and of acting that is not mimetic. It is, of course, impossible to give much idea of the whole of this art on paper. One can only trace out the words of the text and say that they are spoken, or half-sung and chanted, to a fitting and traditional accompaniment of movement and colour, and that they are themselves but half shadows. Yet, despite the difficulties of presentation, I find these words very wonderful, and they become intelligible if, as a friend says, " you read them all the time as though you were listening to music."

If one has the habit of reading plays and imagining their setting, it will not be difficult to imagine the Noh stage—different as it is from our own or even from Western mediaeval stages—and to feel how the incomplete speech is filled out by the music or movement. It is a symbolic stage, a drama of masks—at least they have masks for spirits and gods and young women. It is a theatre of which both Mr. Yeats and Mr. Craig may approve. It is not, like our theatre, a place where every fineness and subtlety must give way ; where every fineness of word or of word-cadence is sacrificed to the " broad effect " ; where the paint must be put on with a broom. It is a stage where every subsidiary art is bent precisely upon holding the faintest shade of a difference ; where the poet may even be silent while the gestures consecrated by four centuries of usage show meaning.

"We work in pure spirit," said Umewaka Minoru, through whose efforts the Noh survived the revolution of 1868, and the fall of the Tokugawa.

Minoru was acting in the Shogun's garden when the news of Perry's arrival stopped the play. Without him the art would have perished. He restored it through poverty and struggle, " living in a poor house, in a poor street, in a kitchen, selling his clothes to buy masks and costumes from the sales of bankrupt companies, and using ' kaiyu ' for rice."

INTRODUCTION

The following prospectus from a programme of one of his later performances (March 1900) will perhaps serve to show the player's attitude toward the play.

Our ancestor was called Umegu Hiogu no Kami Tomotoki. He was the descendant in the ninth generation of Tachibana no Moroye Sadaijin, and lived in Umedzu Yamashiro, hence his family name. After that he lived in Oshima, in the province of Tamba, and died in the fourth year of Ninwa Moroye's descendant, the twenty-second after Tomotoki, was called Hiogu no Kami Tomosato. He was a samurai in Tamba, as his fathers before him. The twenty-eighth descendant was Hiogu no Kami Kagehisa. His mother dreamed that a Noh mask was given from heaven ; she conceived, and Kagehisa was born. From his childhood Kagehisa liked music and dancing, and he was by nature very excellent in both of these arts. The Emperor Gotsuchi Mikado heard his name, and in January in the 13th year of Bunmei he called him to his palace and made him perform the play Ashikari. Kagehisa was then sixteen years old. The Emperor admired him greatly and gave him the decoration (Monsuki) and a curtain which was purple above and white below, and he gave him the honorific ideograph " waka " and thus made him change his name to Umewaka. By the Emperor's order, Ushoben Fugiwara no Shunmei sent the news of

7

this and the gifts to Kagehisa. The letter of the Emperor, given at that time, is still in our house. The curtain was, unfortunately, burned in the great fire of Yedo on the 4th of March in the third year of Bunka. Kagehisa died in the second year of Kioroku and after him the family of Umewaka became professional actors of Noh. Hironaga, the thirtieth descendant of Umewaka Taiyu Rokuro, served Ota Nobunaga.[1] And he was given a territory of 700 koku in Tamba. And he died in Nobunaga's battle, Akechi. His son, Taiyu Rokuro Ujimori, was called to the palace of Tokugawa Iyeyasu in the fourth year of Keicho, and given a territory of 100 koku near his home in Tamba. He died in the third year of Kambun. After that the family of Umewaka served the Tokugawa shoguns with Noh for generation after generation down to the revolution of Meiji (1868). These are the outlines of the genealogy of my house.

This is the 450th anniversary of Tomosato, and so to celebrate him and Kagehisa and Ujimori, we have these performances for three days. We hope that all will come to see them.

The head of the performance is the forty-fifth of his line, the Umewaka Rokoro, and is aided by Umewaka Manzaburo.

(Dated.) In the 33rd year of Meiji, 2nd month.

You see how far this is from the conditions of the Occidental stage. Pride of descent,

---

[1] Nobunaga died in 1582.

INTRODUCTION

pride in having served dynasties now extinct, fragments of ceremony and religious ritual, all serve at first to confuse the modern person, and to draw his mind from the sheer dramatic value of Noh.

Some scholars seem to have added another confusion. They have not understood the function of the individual plays in the performance, and have thought them fragmentary, or have complained of imperfect structure. The Noh plays are often quite complete in themselves ; certain plays are detachable units, comprehensible as single performances, and without annotation or comment. Yet even these can be used as part of the Ban-gumi, the full Noh programme. Certain other plays are only " formed " and intelligible when considered as part of such a series of plays. Again, the texts or libretti of certain other plays, really complete in themselves, seem to us unfinished, because their final scene depends more upon the dance than on the words. The following section of Professor Fenollosa's notes throws a good deal of light on these questions. It is Notebook J, Section I., based on the authority of Mr. Taketi Owada, and runs as follows :

In the time of Tokugawa (A.D. 1602 to 1868), Noh became the music of the Shogun's court and

9

it was called O-no, the programme O-no-gumi, the actor O-no-yakusha, and the stage O-no-butai, with honorific additions. The first ceremony of the year, Utai-zome, was considered very important at the court. In the palaces of the daimyos, also, they had their proper ceremonies. This ceremony of Utai-zome began with the Ashikaga shoguns (in the fourteenth century). At that time on the fourth day of the first month, Kanze (the head of one of the five chartered and hereditary companies of court actors) sang a play in Omaya, and the Shogun gave him jifuku ("clothes of the season"), and this became a custom. In the time of Toyotomi, the second day of the first month was set apart for the ceremony. But in the time of Tokugawa, the third day of the first month was fixed "eternally" as the day for Utai-zome. On that day, at the hour of "tori no jō" (about 5 A.M.), the Shogun presented himself in a large hall in Hon-Maru (where the imperial palace now is), taking with him the San-ke, or three relative daimyos, the ministers, and all the other daimyos and officials, all dressed in the robes called "noshime-kami-shimo." And the "Tayus" (or heads) of the Kanze and Komparu schools of acting come every year, and the Tayus of Hosho and Kita on alternate years, and the Waki actors, that is, the actors of second parts, and the actors of Kiogen or farces, and the hayashikata ("cats," or musicians) and the singers of the chorus, all bow down on the verandah of the third hall dressed in robes called "suo," and in hats called "yeboshi."

INTRODUCTION

And while the cup of the Shogun is poured out three times, Kanze sings the " Shikai-nami " passage from the play of Takasago, still bowing. Then the plays Oi-matsu, Tōbuku, and Takasago are sung with music, and when they are over the Shogun gives certain robes, called the " White-aya," with crimson lining, to the three chief actors, and robes called " orikami " to the other actors. Then the three chief actors put on the new robes over their " suos " and begin at once to dance the Dance of the Match of Bows and Arrows. And the chant that accompanies it is as follows :

The chief actor sings—

" Shakuson, Shakuson ! " (Buddha, Buddha !)

And the chorus sings this rather unintelligible passage—

" Taking the bow of Great Love and the arrow of Wisdom, he awakened Sandoku from sleep. Aisemmyō-o displayed these two as the symbols of IN and YO.[1] Monju (another deity) appeared in the form of Yo-yu and caught the serpent, Kishu-ja, and made it into a bow. From its eyes he made him his arrows.[2]

" The Empress Jingō of our country defeated the rebels with these arrows and brought the peace of Ciyo-shun to the people. O Hachiman Daibosatsu, Emperor Ojin, War-god Yumi-ya, enshrined in Iwa-

---

[1] [In and yo are divisions of metric, and there is a Pythagorean-like symbolism attached to them.]

[2] [The serpent is presumably the sky, and the stars the eyes made into arrows.]

shimidzu, where the clear water-spring flows out !
O, O, O !   This water is water flowing forever."

This "yumi-ya" text cannot be used any-
where save in this ceremony at the Shogun's
court, and in the "Takigi-No" of the Kasuga
temple at Nara (where a few extra lines are
interpolated).

When the above chant and dance are
finished, the Shogun takes the robe "Kata-
ginu" from his shoulders and throws it to the
samurai in attendance.   The samurai hands it to
the minister, who walks with it to the verandah
and presents it to the Taiyu of Kanze very
solemnly.   Then all the daimyos present take
off their "kata-ginus" and give them to the
chief actors, and thus ends the ceremony of
Utai-zome.   The next day the tayus, or chief
actors, take the robes back to the daimyos and
get money in exchange for them.

There are performances of Noh lasting five
days at the initiations, marriages, and the like,
of the Shoguns ; and at the Buddhist memorial
services for dead Shoguns for four days.   There
are performances for the reception of imperial
messengers from Kyoto, at which the actors
have to wear various formal costumes.   On
one day of the five-day performances the town
people of the eight hundred and eight streets

of Yedo are admitted, and they are marshalled by the officers of every street. The nanushi, or street officers, assemble the night before by the gates of Ote and Kikyo, and each officer carries aloft a paper lantern bearing the name of his street. They take sake and refreshments and wait for the dawn. It looks like a place on fire, or like a camp before battle.

The Kanze method of acting was made the official style of the Tokugawa Shoguns, and the tayus, or chief actors, of Kanze were placed at the head of all Noh actors. To the Kanze tayu alone was given the privilege of holding one subscription performance, or Kanjin-No, during his lifetime, for the space of ten days. And for this performance he had the right to certain dues and levies on the daimyos and on the streets of the people of Yedo. The daimyos were not allowed to attend the common theatre, but they could go to the Kanjin-No. (Note that the common theatre, the place of mimicry and direct imitation of life, has always been looked down upon in Japan. The Noh, the symbolic and ritual stage, is a place of honour to actor and audience alike.) The daimyos and even their wives and daughters could see Kanjin-No without staying behind the blinds. Programmes were sold in the streets, and a drum was beaten as a signal, as is still done to get an audience for the wrestling matches.

The privilege of holding one subscription performance was later granted to the Hosho company also.

Ban-gumi

In the performance of Utai, or Noh, the arrangement of pieces for the day is called " Ban-gumi." " Gumi " means a setting in order, and " Ban " is derived from the old term " Ban-no-mai," which was formerly used when the two kinds of mai, or dancing, the Korean " u-ho " and the Chinese " sa-ho," were performed one after the other.

Now the Ka-den-sho, or secret book of Noh, decrees that the arrangement of plays shall be as follows :

A " Shugen " must come first. And Shugen, or congratulatory pieces, are limited to Noh of the Gods (that is, to pieces connected with some religious rite), because this country of the rising sun is the country of the gods. The gods have guarded the country from Kami-yo (the age of the gods) down to the time of the present reign. So in praise of them and in prayer we perform first this Kami-No.

The Shura, or battle-piece, comes second, for the gods and emperors pacified this country with bows and arrows ; therefore, to defeat and put out

INTRODUCTION

the devils, we perform the Shura.   (That is to say,
it is sympathetic magic.)

Kazura, or Onna-mono, "wig-pieces," or pieces for
females, come third.   Many think that any Kazura
will do, but it must be a " female Kazura," for after
battle comes peace, or Yu-gen, mysterious calm, and
in time of peace the cases of love come to pass.   More-
over, the battle-pieces are limited to men; so we now
have the female piece in contrast like in and yo (the
different divisions of the metric, before mentioned).

The fourth piece is Oni-No, or the Noh of spirits.
After battle comes peace and glory, but they soon
depart in their turn.   The glory and pleasures of
man are not reliable at all.   Life is like a dream and
goes with the speed of lightning.   It is like a dew-
drop in the morning; it soon falls and is broken.
To suggest these things and to lift up the heart for
Buddha (to produce " Bodai-shin ") we have this
sort of play after the Onna-mono, that is, just after
the middle of the programme, when some of the
audience will be a little tired.   Just to wake them
out of their sleep we have these plays of spirits
(" Oni ").   Here are shown the struggles and the
sins of mortals, and the audience, even while they sit
for pleasure, will begin to think about Buddha and
the coming world.   It is for this reason that Noh is
called Mu-jin-Kyo, the immeasurable scripture.[1]

---

[1] These pieces are the most interesting because of their profound and subtle psychology and because of situations entirely
foreign to our Western drama, if not to our folk-lore and legend.
—E. P.

Fifth comes a piece which has some bearing upon the moral duties of man, Jin, Gi, Rei, Chi, Shin; that is, Compassion, Righteousness, Politeness, Wisdom, and Faithfulness. This fifth piece teaches the duties of man here in this world as the fourth piece represents the results of carelessness to such duties.

Sixth comes another Shugen, or congratulatory piece, as conclusion to the whole performance, to congratulate and call down blessings on the lords present, the actors themselves, and the place. To show that though the spring may pass, still there is a time of its return, this Shugen is put in again just as at the beginning.

This is what is written in the Ka-den-sho. Then some one, I think Mr. Owada, comments as follows :

Though it is quite pedantic in wording, still the order of the performance is always like this. To speak in a more popular manner, first comes the Noh of the Divine Age (Kamiyo); then the battle-piece; then the play of women; fourth, the pieces which have a very quiet and deep interest, to touch the audience to their very hearts; fifth, the pieces which have stirring or lively scenes; and, sixth, pieces which praise the lords and the reign.

This is the usual order. When we have five pieces instead of six, we sing at the end of the performance the short passage from the play Takasago, beginning at " Senshuraku wa tami wo nade,"

INTRODUCTION

" Make the people glad with the joy of a Thousand Autumns." (From the final chorus of Takasago.) This is called the " adding Shugen." But if in the fifth piece there are phrases like " Medeta kere " or " Hisashi kere "—" Oh, how happy ! " or " O everlasting,"—then there is no necessity to sing the extra passage. In performances in memory of the dead, Tsuizen-No, they sing short passages from Toru and Naniwa.

Though five or six pieces are the usual number, there can be more or even fewer pieces, in which case one must use the general principles of the above schedule in designing and arranging the programme.

I think I have quoted enough to make clear one or two points.

First : There has been in Japan from the beginning a clear distinction between serious and popular drama. The merely mimetic stage has been despised.

Second : The Noh holds up a mirror to nature in a manner very different from the Western convention of plot. I mean the Noh performance of the five or six plays in order presents a complete service of life. We do not find, as we find in Hamlet, a certain situation or problem set out and analysed. The Noh service presents, or symbolizes, a complete diagram of life and recurrence.

The individual pieces treat for the most

part known situations, in a manner analogous to that of the Greek plays, in which we find, for instance, a known Oedipus in a known predicament.

Third : As the tradition of Noh is unbroken, we find in the complete performance numerous elements which have disappeared from our Western stage ; that is, morality plays, religious mysteries, and even dances—like those of the mass—which have lost what we might call their dramatic significance.

Certain texts of Noh will therefore be interesting only to students of folk-lore or of comparative religion. The battle-pieces will present little of interest, because Chansons de Geste are pretty much the same all the world over. The moralities are on a par with Western moralities, for ascetic Buddhism and ascetic Christianity have about the same set of preach-ments. These statements are general and admit of numerous exceptions, but the lover of the stage and the lover of drama and of poetry will find his chief interest in the psychological pieces, or the Plays of Spirits ; the plays that are, I think, more Shinto than Buddhist. These plays are full of ghosts, and the ghost psychology is amazing. The parallels with Western spiritist doctrines are very curious.

INTRODUCTION

This is, however, an irrelevant or extraneous interest, and one might set it aside if it were not bound up with a dramatic and poetic interest of the very highest order.

I think I can now give a couple of texts, without much more preface than saying that the stage is visible from three sides. It is reached by a bridge which is divided into three sections by three real pine trees which are small and in pots. There is one scene painted on the background. It is a pine tree, the symbol of the unchanging. It is painted right on the back of the stage, and, as this cannot be shifted, it remains the same for all plays.

A play very often represents some one going a journey. The character walks along the bridge or about the stage, announces where he is and where he is going, and often explains the meaning of his symbolic gestures, or tells what the dance means, or why one is dancing.

Thus, in Sotoba Komachi, a play by Kiyotsugu, two priests are going from Koyosan to Kioto, and in Settsu they meet with Ono no Komachi ; that is to say, they meet with what appears to be an old woman sitting on a roadside shrine—though she is really the wraith of Ono, long dead.

SOTOBA KOMACHI

Ono

When I was young I had pride
And the flowers in my hair
Were like spring willows.
I spoke like the nightingales, and now am old,
Old by a hundred years, and wearied out.
I will sit down and rest.

The Waki
*(one of the priests, is shocked at her impiety
and says)*

It is near evening; let us be getting along.
Now will you look at that beggar. She is
sitting on a sotoba (*a carved wooden devotional
stick, or shrine*). Tell her to come off it and sit
on some proper thing.

Ono

Eh, for all your blather it has no letters
on it, not a smudge of old painting. I thought
it was only a stick.

'NOH'

WAKI

Is it only a stick or a stump? May be it had once fine flowers—in its time, in its time; and now it is a stick, to be sure, with the blessed Buddha cut in it.

ONO

Oh, well then, I'm a stump, too, and well buried, with a flower at my heart. Go on and talk of the shrine.

The Tsure, in this case the second priest, tells the legend of the shrine, and while he is doing it, the Waki notices something strange about the old hag, and cries out—
Who are you?

ONO

I am the ruins of Ono,
The daughter of Ono no Yoshizane.

WAKI and TSURE
(*together*)

How sad a ruin is this:
Komachi was in her day a bright flower;
She had the blue brows of Katsura;
She used no powder at all;
She walked in beautiful raiment in palaces.

SOTOBA KOMACHI

Many attended her verse in our speech
And in the speech of the foreign court.

[That is, China.]

White of winter is over her head,
Over the husk of her shoulders ;
Her eyes are no more like the colour on distant
    mountains.
She is like a dull moon that fades in the dawn's
    grip.
The wallet about her throat has in it a few
    dried beans,
A bundle is wrapped on her back, and on her
    shoulder is a basket of woven roots ;
She cannot hide it at all.
She is begging along the road ;
She wanders, a poor, daft shadow.

[*I cannot quite make out whether the priest is
still sceptical, and thinks he has before him merely
an old woman who thinks she is Komachi. At any
rate, she does not want commiseration, and
replies.*]

ONO

Daft ! Will you hear him ? In my own
young days I had a hundred letters from men
a sight better than he is. They came like
rain-drops in May. And I had a high head,
may be, that time. And I sent out no answer.

You think because you see me alone now that
I was in want of a handsome man in the old
days, when Shosho came with the others—Shii
no Shosho of Fukakusa [Deep Grass] that
came to me in the moonlight and in the dark
night and in the nights flooded with rain, and
in the black face of the wind and in the wild
swish of the snow. He came as often as the
melting drops fall from the eaves, ninety-nine
times, and he died. And his ghost is about me,
driving me on with the madness.

———

Umewaka Minoru acted Ono in this play
on March 8, 1899. It is quite usual for an
old actor, wearing a mask, to take the part of
a young woman. There is another play of
Ono and Shosho called Kayoi Komachi, " Komachi Going " ; it is by a Minoru, and Umewaka
acted it on November 19, 1899 ; and it was
followed by Suma Genji. I shall give both of
these plays complete without further comment.

TECHNICAL TERMS IN NOH

Shite (pronounced " *Sch'tay* ") : The hero or chief
  character.
Tsure : The follower of the hero.
Waki : Guest or guests, very often a wandering
  priest.
Waki no tsure, or *Wadzure* : Guest's attendant.
Tomo : An insignificant attendant.
Kogata : A very young boy.
Kiogenshi : Sailor or servant.
Hannya : An evil spirit.

The speaking part of Noh is called " Kataru,"
the singing parts " Utai."

KAYOI KOMACHI [1]

The Scene is in Yamashiro

CHARACTERS

SHITE, SHOSHO, the ghost of ONO NO KOMACHI'S
lover.
WAKI, or subsidiary character, a priest.
TSURE, Ono no Komachi.

WAKI

I am a priest in the village of Yase. And
there's an odd little woman comes here every
day with fruit and fuel. If she comes to-day
I shall ask her who she is.

[1] [NOTE.—The crux of the play is that Shosho would not
accept Buddhism, and thus his spirit and Ono's are kept apart.
There is nothing like a ghost for holding to an idée fixe. In
Nishikigi, the ghosts of the two lovers are kept apart because the
woman had steadily refused the hero's offering of charm sticks.
The two ghosts are brought together by the piety of a wandering
priest. Mr. Yeats tells me that he has found a similar legend in
Arran, where the ghosts come to a priest to be married.—E. P.]

27

'NOH'

Tsure

(announcing herself to the audience)

I am a woman who lives out about Itchiharano. There are many rich houses in Yase, and I take fruit and wood to them, and there's where I'm going now.

Waki

Then you are the woman. What sort of fruit have you there?

Tsure

I've nuts and kaki and chestnuts and plums and peaches, and big and little oranges, and a bunch of tachibana, which reminds me of days that are gone.

Waki

Then that's all right—but who are you?

Tsure

(*To herself.*) I can't tell him that now. (*To him.*) I'm just a woman who lives out by Ichihara-no-be, in all that wild grass there.

[*So saying she disappears.*

KAYOI KOMACHI

WAKI

That's queer. I asked her her name. She won't tell me. She says she's just a woman from Ichihara, and then she's gone like a mist. If you go down by Ichihara you can hear the wind in the Susuki bushes as in the poem of Ono no Komachi's, where she says, " Ono, no I will not tell the wind my name is Ono, as long as Susuki has leaves." I dare say it is she or her spirit. I will go there the better to pray for her.

CHORUS
(announcing the action and change of scene)

So he went out of his little cottage in the temple enclosure. He went to Ichihara and prayed.

TSURE
(her voice heard from the furze bush, speaking to the priest)

There's a heap of good in your prayers ; do you think you could bring me to Buddha ?

SHITE
(the spirit of SHOSHO)

It's an ill time to do that. Go back. You move in ill hours.

'NOH'

TSURE

I say they were very fine prayers. I will not come back without a struggle.

SHITE

I've a sad heart to see you looking up to Buddha, you who left me alone, I diving in the black rivers of hell. Will soft prayers be a comfort to you in your quiet heaven, you who know that I'm alone in that wild, desolate place? To put you away from me! That's all he has come for, with his prayers. Will they do any good to my sort?

TSURE

O dear, you can speak for yourself, but my heart is clear as new moonlight.

CHORUS

See, she comes out of the bush.
[*That is, the spirit has materialized.*]

SHITE

Will nothing make you turn back?

KAYOI KOMACHI

Tsure

Faith is like a wild deer on the mountain.
It will not stop when you call it.

Shite

Then I'll be the dog of your Buddha ; I
will not be beaten away from you.

Tsure

How terrible, how terrible his face is ! [1]

Chorus

See, he has caught at her sleeve.

Waki

(*This apparently trivial speech of the* Waki's
*arrests them. It is most interesting in view of
the " new " doctrine of the suggestibility or
hypnotizability of ghosts. The* Waki *says
merely :*) Are you Ono no Komachi ? And
you, Shosho ? Did you court her a hundred
nights ? Can you show this ?
    [*Then they begin the dance of this Noh,
    the image of the coming of* Shosho.

---

[1] Shosho is not by any means bringing a humble and contrite
heart to his conversion.

31

'NOH'

TSURE

I did not know you had such deep thirst
for me.

SHITE

You deceived me by telling me to drive
out a hundred nights. I thought you meant
it. I took my carriage and came.

TSURE

I said, " Change your appearance, or people
will see you and talk."

SHITE

I changed my carriage. Though I had
fresh horses in Kohata, I even came barefoot.

TSURE

You came in every sort of condition.

SHITE

It was not such a dark way by moonlight.

TSURE

You even came in the snow.

KAYOI KOMACHI

Shite

I can, even now, seem to be shaking it off
my sleeves.
    [*This movement is developed into a dance.*

Tsure

In the evening rain.

Shite

That devil in your rain was my invisible
terror.

Tsure

On the night when there was no cloud——

Shite

I had my own rain of tears ; that was the
dark night, surely.

Tsure

The twilight was always my terror.

Shite

She will wait for the moon, I said, but she
will never wait for me.

'NOH'

Chorus

The dawn ! oh, the dawn is also a time of many thoughts.

Shite

Yes, for me.

Chorus

Though the fowls crow, though the bells ring, and though the night shall never come up, it is less than nothing to her.

Shite

With many struggles——

Chorus

—I went for ninety-nine nights. And this is the hundredth night. This night is the longing fulfilled. He hurries. What is he wearing ?

Shite

His kasa is wretched ; it is a very poor cloak, indeed.

Chorus

His hat is in tatters.

KAYOI KOMACHI

SHITE

His under-coat is in rags.
[*All this refers both to* SHOSHO'S *having
come disguised, and being now in but
the tatters of some sort of astral body.
Then presumably a light shows in his
spirit, as probably he had worn some
rich garment under his poor disguise.*

CHORUS

He comes in the dress with patterns ;
He comes oversprinkled with flowers.
It is Shosho !

SHITE

In a garment with many folds.

CHORUS

The violet-coloured hakama.   He thought
she would wait for his coming.

SHITE

I hurried to her as now.

CHORUS
(*speaking for* SHOSHO'S *thoughts*)

Though she only asks me to drink a cup of

35

moonlight, I will not take it. It is a trick to catch one for Buddha.

CHORUS
(in a final statement)

Both their sins vanished. They both became pupils of Buddha, both Komachi and Shosho.

THE END

The final dance means that the lovers are spirits fluttering in the grass.

This eclogue is very incomplete. Ono seems rather like Echo, and without the last two lines of the chorus one could very well imagine her keeping up her tenzone with Shosho until the end of time.

In the performance of November 19, as stated before, this play was followed by Manza-buro's Suma Genji (Genji at Suma).

I must ask the reader to suspend his judgment of the dramatic values of such plays until he has read Nishikigi and some of the longer eclogues, at least some of those in which the utai or libretto set by itself conveys a fuller sense of the meaning.

SUMA GENJI

CHARACTERS

SHITE, an old wood-cutter, who is an apparition of
the hero, GENJI, as a sort of place-spirit, the
spirit of the seashore at Suma.

WAKI, FUJIWARA, a priest with a hobby for folk-lore,
who is visiting sacred places.

SECOND SHITE, or the SHITE in his second manner
or apparition, GENJI's spirit appearing in a sort
of glory of waves and moonlight.

WAKI
(announcing himself)

I, Fujiwara no Okinori,
Am come over the sea from Hiuga ;
I am a priest from the shinto temple at Miya-
zaki,
And, as I lived far afield,
I could not see the temple of the great god at
Ise ;
And now I am a-mind to go thither,
And am come to Suma, the sea-board.

Here Genji lived, and here I shall see the young
    cherry,
The tree that is so set in the tales——

SHITE

And I am a wood-cutter of Suma.
I fish in the twilight ;
By day I pack wood and make salt.
Here is the mount of Suma.
There is the tree, the young cherry.[1]

And you may be quite right about Genji's
having lived here. That blossom will flare
in a moment.[2]

WAKI

I must find out what that old man knows.
(*To* SHITE.) Sir, you seem very poor, and
yet you neglect your road ; you stop on your
way home, just to look at a flower. Is that
the tree of the stories ?

SHITE

I dare say I'm poor enough ; but you

---

[1] It must be remembered that the properties and scene are
not representational but symbolic, the hero-actor simply says in
effect, " Pretend that that is the tree and that the mountain."

[2] There is here the double-entente. The blossom will really
come out : it is a day of anniversary or something of that kind ;
also Genji will appear in his proper glory, as the audience
knows, though the Waki does not.

don't know much if you're asking about that
tree, " Is it the fine tree of Suma ? "

WAKI

Well, *is* it the tree ?   I've come on purpose
to see it.

SHITE

What ! you really have come to see the
cherry-blossom, and not to look at Mount
Suma ?

WAKI

Yes ; this is where Genji lived, and you
are so old that you ought to know a lot of
stories about him.

CHORUS
(*telling out* GENJI'S *thoughts*)

If I tell over the days that are gone,
My sleeves will wither.[1]
The past was at Kiritsubo ;
I went to the lovely cottage, my mother's,
But the emperor loved me.

I was made esquire at twelve, with the hat.
The soothsayers unrolled my glories.[2]   I was

---

[1] That is, this present manifestation in the shape of an old
man will fade.

[2] The " soothsayer " is literally " the physiognomist from
Corea."

called Hikaru Genji. I was chujo in Hahakigi province. I was chujo in the land of the maple-feasting.[1] At twenty-five I came to Suma, knowing all sorrow of seafare, having none to attend my dreams, no one to hear the old stories.

Then I was recalled to the city. I passed from office to office. I was naidaijin in Miwotsu-kushi, I was dajodaijin in the lands of Otome, and daijotenno in Fuji no Uraba ; for this I was called Hikam Kimi.

Waki

But tell me exactly where he lived. Tell me all that you know about him.

Shite

One can't place the exact spot ; he·lived all along here by the waves. If you will wait for the moonlight you might see it all in a mist.

Chorus

He was in Suma in the old days——

Shite

(*stepping behind a screen or making some sign of departure, he completes the sentence of the chorus*) —but now in the aery heaven.

---

[1] Chujo, naidaijin, etc. are names for different grades of office.

SUMA GENJI

Chorus

(*to* Waki)

Wait and the moon will show him.
That woodman is gone in the clouds.

Waki

That " woodman " was Genji himself, who
was here talking live words. I will wait for
the night. I will stay here to see what happens.
(*Announcing his act.*[1]) Then Fujiwara no Okinori lay down and heard the waves filled with
music.

Scene II. *begins with the appearance of the*
Second Shite, *that is to say, a bright apparition
of* Genji *in supernatural form.*

Genji

How beautiful this sea is ! When I trod
the grass here I was called " Genji the gleaming," and now from the vaulting heaven I
reach down to set a magic on mortals. I sing
of the moon in this shadow, here on this sea-

---

[1] The characters often give their own stage directions or
explain the meaning of their acts, as in the last line here.

4I

marge of Suma.   Here I will dance Sei-kai-ha,
the blue dance of the sea waves.

> [*And then he begins to dance.*

CHORUS
(*accompanying and describing the dance*)

The flower of waves-reflected
Is on his white garment ;
That pattern covers the sleeve.
The air is alive with flute-sounds,
With the song of various pipes
The land is a-quiver,
And even the wild sea of Suma
Is filled with resonant quiet.

Moving in clouds and in rain,
The dream overlaps with the real ;
There was a light out of heaven,
There was a young man at the dance here ;
Surely it was Genji Hikaru,
It was Genji Hikaru in spirit.

GENJI

My name is known to the world ;
Here by the white waves was my dwelling ;
But I am come down out of sky
To put my glamour on mortals.

SUMA GENJI

CHORUS

Gracious is the presence of Genji,
It is like the feel of things at Suma.

GENJI
(referring also to a change in the dance)

The wind is abated.

CHORUS

A thin cloud——

GENJI

—clings to the clear-blown sky.
It seems like the spring-time.

CHORUS

He came down like Brahma, Indra, and the
    Four Kings visiting the abode of Devas
    and Men.[1]
He, the soul of the place.[2]
He, who seemed but a woodman,
He flashed with the honoured colours,
He the true-gleaming.

[1] The Four Kings, i.e. of the four points of the compass.
Devas (spirits) and Men occupy the position immediately below
the Gods.

[2] More precisely " He became the place." You can compare
this with Buckle, or Jules Romains' studies in unanimism.

43

'NOH'

Blue-grey is the garb they wear here,
Blue-grey he fluttered in Suma ;
His sleeves were like the grey sea-waves ;
They moved with curious rustling,
Like the noise of the restless waves,
Like the bell of a country town
'Neath the nightfall.

THE END

I dare say the play, Suma Genji, will seem undramatic to some people the first time they read it. The suspense is the suspense of waiting for a supernatural manifestation—which comes. Some will be annoyed at a form of psychology which is, in the West, relegated to spiritistic séances. There is, however, no doubt that such psychology exists. All through the winter of 1914–15 I watched Mr. Yeats correlating folk-lore (which Lady Gregory had collected in Irish cottages) and data of the occult writers, with the habits of charlatans of Bond Street. If the Japanese authors had not combined the psychology of such matters with what is to me a very fine sort of poetry, I would not bother about it.

The reader will miss the feel of suspense if

44

he is unable to put himself in sympathy with the priest eager to see "even in a vision" the beauty lost in the years, "the shadow of the past in bright form." I do not say that this sympathy is easily acquired. It is too unusual a frame of mind for us to fall into it without conscious effort. But if one can once get over the feeling of hostility, if one can once let himself into the world of the Noh, there is undoubtedly a new beauty before him. I have found it well worth the trial, and can hope that others will also.

The arrangement of five or six Noh into one performance explains, in part, what may seem like a lack of construction in some of the pieces ; the plays have, however, a very severe construction of their own, a sort of musical construction.

When a text seems to "go off into nothing" at the end, the reader must remember "that the vagueness or paleness of words is made good by the emotion of the final dance," for the Noh has its unity in emotion. It has also what we may call Unity of Image.[1] At least,

---

[1] This intensification of the Image, this manner of construction, is very interesting to me personally, as an Imagiste, for we Imagistes knew nothing of these plays when we set out in our own manner. These plays are also an answer to a question that has several times been put to me : "Could one do a long Imagiste poem, or even a long poem in vers libre ?"

the better plays are all built into the intensification of a single Image : the red maple leaves and the snow flurry in Nishikigi, the pines in Takasago, the blue-grey waves and wave pattern in Suma Genji, the mantle of feathers in the play of that name, Hagoromo.

When it comes to presenting Professor Fenollosa's records of his conversations with Umewaka Minoru, the restorer of Noh, I find myself much puzzled as to where to begin. I shall, however, plunge straight into the conversation of May 15, 1900, as that seems germane to other matters already set forth in this excerpt, preceding it only by the quaint record of an earlier meeting, December 20, 1898, as follows :

Called on old Mr. Umewaka with Mr. Hirata. Presented him with large box of eggs. He thanked me for presenting last Friday 18 yen to Takeyo for my six lessons, which began on November 18. I apologized to him for the mistake of years ago, thanked him for his frankness, his reticence to others, and his kindness in allowing me to begin again with him, asked him to receive 15 yen as a present in consideration of his recent help.

He was very affable, and talked with me for about 1½ hours. He asked me to sing, and I sang "Hansakaba." He praised me, said everything was exactly right and said that both he and

SUMA GENJI

Takeyo considered my progress wonderful; better than a Japanese could make. He said I was already advanced enough to sing in a Japanese company.[1]

Mosse and I are the only foreigners who have ever been taught Noh, and I am the only foreigner now practising it.

We spoke much of the art of it, I giving him a brief account of Greek drama. He already knew something about opera.

He said the excellence of Noh lay in emotion, not in action or externals. Therefore there were no accessories, as in the theatres. " Spirit " (tamashii) was the word he used. The pure spirit was what it (Noh) worked in, so it was higher than other arts. If a Noh actor acted his best, Umewaka could read his character. The actor could not conceal it. The spirit must out, the " whole man," he said. Therefore he always instructed his sons to be moral, pure and true in all their daily lives, otherwise they could not become the greatest actors.

He spoke much about the (popular) theatre, of its approximation of Noh when he was about thirteen years old. The present Danjuro's father and his troop disguised themselves and came to the performance of Kanjin Noh, from which they were normally excluded. This was the one opportunity for the public to see Noh, it is (as said elsewhere) the single

---

[1] This is in Fenollosa's diary, not in a part of a lecture or in anything he had published, so there is no question of its being an immodest statement.

47

benefit performance allowed to each master Noh actor. Other actors were excluded.

Then it was that Ichikawa, having seen these Noh plays, imitated them in the famous " Kanjiinjo," which the present Danjuro still plays as one of his 18 special pieces. Under the present regime, the popular actors have access to the Noh plays, and the popular plays have imitated them still further. Almost all forms of music and recitation have now (1898) taken more or less of their style from Noh.

Noh has been a purification of the Japanese soul for 400 years. Kobori Enshu classified the fifteen virtues of Noh, among which he counted mental and bodily health as one, calling it " Healing without medicine."

" Dancing is especially known, by its circulation of the blood, to keep off the disease of old age."

Now Minoru and his sons occasionally go to Danjuro's theatre. He spoke much about the Shogun's court. When a Noh actor was engaged by the Shogun he had to sign long articles to the effect that he would never divulge even to his wife or his relatives any of the doings or descriptions of things in the palace, also that he would not visit houses of pleasure or go to the theatre. If caught doing these things he was severely punished. Occasionally a Noh actor would go to the theatre in disguise.

With the exception of the Kanjin Noh, common people could not, at that time, see the Noh, but a very few were occasionally let in to the monthly rehearsals.

SUMA GENJI

The notes for May 15, 1900, begin as follows :

He (Minoru) says that Mitsuni (a certain actor) has learning and great Nesshin, or technique, but that, after all the technique is learned, the great difficulty is to grasp the spirit of the piece.

He always tells the newspaper men to-day not to write criticisms of Noh. They can criticize the popular theatre, for there even the plots may change, and amateurs can judge it. But in Noh everything comes down by tradition from early Tokugawa days and cannot be judged by any living man, but can only be followed faithfully.[1]

Although there is no general score for actors and cats (i.e. the four musicians who have sat at the back of the Noh stage for so many centuries that no one quite knows what they mean or how they came there), there is in the hands of the Taiyu, or actor-manager, a roll such as he (Minoru) himself has, which gives general directions, not much detail. This contains only the ordinary text, with no special notations for singing, but for the dances there are minute diagrams showing where to stand, how far to go forward, the turns in a circle, the turns to right or left, how far to go with the right or left foot, how many steps, eyes right, eyes left, what mask and what clothes are to be worn, the very

---

[1] This is not so stupid as it seems ; we might be fairly grateful if some private or chartered company had preserved the exact Elizabethan tradition for acting Shakespeare.

lines in which the clothes must hang, and the exact position of the arms. There are drawings of figures naked for old men, women, girls, boys, ghosts, and all kinds of characters sitting and standing; they show the proper relation of limbs and body. Then there are similar drawings of the same figures clothed.

But one cannot trust merely to such a set of instructions. There is a great deal that must be supplied by experience, feeling, and tradition, and which has always been so supplied. Minoru feels this so strongly that he has not yet shown the rolls to his sons, for fear it might make them mechanical.

"KUDEN" (TRADITION)

A book of this sort has been handed down by his ancestors from early Tokugawa days, but it is only a rough draft. He has written a long supplement on the finer points, but has shown it to no one. One should not trust to it, either. Such fine things as Matsukaze, the pose for looking at the moon, or at the dawn, or at the double reflection of the moon in two tubs, and all the detail of business cannot be written down; at such places he writes merely " kuden " (tradition), to show that this is something that can be learned only from a master. Sometimes his teacher used to beat him with a fan when he was learning.

Relying on record plus such tradition, we can say with fair certitude that there has been no appreciable change in Noh since the early days of Tokugawa (that is to say, since the beginning of the seventeenth century, or about the end of Shakespeare's lifetime).

Kuden, or this feeling for the traditional intensity, is not to be gained by mere teaching or mimicry, or by a hundred times trying; but it must be learned by a grasp of the inner spirit. In a place, for instance, where a father comes to his lost son, walks three steps forward, pats him twice on the head and balances his stick, it is very difficult to get all this into grace and harmony, and it certainly cannot be written down or talked into a man by word of mouth.

Imitation must not be wholly external. There is a tradition of a young actor who wished to learn Sekidera Komachi, the most secret and difficult of the three plays, which alone are so secret that they were told and taught only by father to eldest son. He followed a fine old woman, eighty years of age, in the street and watched her every step. After a while she was alarmed and asked him why he was following her. He said she was interesting. She replied that she was too old. Then he confessed that he was an ambitious Noh actor and wanted to play Komachi.

An ordinary woman would have praised him, but she did not. She said it was bad for Noh, though it might be good for the common theatre, to imitate facts. For Noh he must feel the thing as a whole, from the inside. He would not get it copying facts point by point. All this is true.

'NOH'

You must lay great stress upon this in explaining the meaning and aesthetics of the Noh.

There is a special medium for expressing emotion. It is the voice.

Each pupil has his own voice ; it cannot be made to imitate the voice of an old woman or a spirit (oni). It must remain always the same, his own ; yet with that one individual voice of his he must so express himself as to make it clear that it is the mentality of an old woman, or whatever it happens to be, who is speaking.

It is a Noh saying that " The heart is the form."

Costumes

There is a general tradition as to costumes. Coloured garments cannot be interchanged for white. The general colour is a matter of record, but not the minute patterns, which may be changed from time to time. It is not necessary that one dress should be reserved for one particular character in one particular piece. Even in Tokugawa days there was not always a costume for each special character. Some were used for several parts and some were unique ; so also were the masks.

The general colour and colour-effect of the dress cannot be changed : say it were small circular patterns on a black ground, this must remain, but the exact flower or ornament inside the circles may vary. The length and cut of the sleeve could not be altered, but only the small details of the pattern.

SUMA GENJI

The size of the pattern might be changed just a little.

MASKS

The hannia, or daemonic masks, are different. The hannia in Awoi no Uye is lofty in feeling; that of Dojoji is base. They are very different. The masks of Shunkan, Semimaru, Kagekiyo, and Yoroboshi cannot be used for any other parts. Kontan's mask can be used for several parts, as, for example, the second shite in Takasago. Of course if one has only one hannia mask one must use it for all hannia, but it is better not to do so. The Adachiga-hara hannia is the lowest in feeling.

Fifty years ago they tried to copy the old masks exactly. The Shogun had Kanze's masks copied even to the old spots. Now it is difficult to get good sculptors.

Turning the head is very difficult, for the actor must be one piece with the mask.

An ordinary mask is worth 30 yen; a great one, 200. At first one cannot distinguish between them. But the longer you look at a good mask the more charged with life it becomes. A common actor cannot use a really good mask. He cannot make himself one with it. A great actor makes it live.

MUSIC

In the notes for a conversation of May 6, there are the following remarks about the singing or chanting [the Noh texts are part in prose and part in verse ; some parts are sung and some spoken, or one might better say, intoned] :

The importance of the music is in its intervals [he seems to mean intervals between beats, i.e. rhythm intervals, not " intervals " of pitch]. It is just like the dropping of rain from the eaves.

The musical bar is a sort of double bar made up of five notes and seven notes, or of seven notes and then seven more notes, the fourteen notes being sung in the same time as the twelve first ones.

The division of seven syllables is called " yo," that of five is called " in " ; the big drum is called " yo," and the small drum " in." The seven syllables are the part of the big drum, the five syllables are the part of the small drum—but if they come in succession it is too regular ; so sometimes they reverse and the big drum takes the " in " part and the small drum the " yo."

The head of the chorus naturally controls the musicians. The chorus is called " kimi," or lord, and the " cats," or musicians, are called " subjects." When Minoru acts as head of the chorus, he says he can manage the " cats " by a prolonging or shortening of sounds. [This is obscure, but apparently each musician has ideas of his own about tempo.]

The " cats " must conform to him. The chorus

is subject to the shite, or chief actor. A certain number of changes may have crept into the tradition. The art consists in not being mechanical. The " cats," the chorus, and the shite " feel out their own originality," and render their own emotions. Even during the last fifteen years some changes may have crept in unconsciously. Even in Tokugawa days there never was any general score bringing all the parts under a single eye. There is not and never has been any such score. There are independent traditions. [NOTE.—The privileges of acting as "cats" and as waki were hereditary privileges of particular families, just as the privilege of acting the chief parts pertained to the members of the five hereditary schools.] Minoru and other actors may know the parts [he means here the musical air] instinctively or by memory; no one has ever written them down. Some actors know only the arias of the few pieces of which they are masters.

Each " cat " of each school has his own traditions. When he begins to learn, he writes down in his note-book a note for each one of the twelve syllables. Each man has his own notation, and he has a more or less complete record to learn from. These details are never told to any one. The ordinary actors and chorus singers do not know them.

In singing, everything depends on the most minute distinction between " in " and " yo." Minoru was surprised to hear that this was not so in

the West. In "yo" there must be "in," and in
"in," "yo." This adds breadth and softness,
"haba" he calls it.[1]

The Stage

The stage is, as I have said, a platform open
on three sides and reached by a bridge from
the green-room. The notes on the conversation of June 2 run as follows :

They have Hakama Noh in summer. The general
audience does not like it, but experts can see the
movements better as the actors sometimes wear no
upper dress at all, and are naked save for the semi-
transparent hakama. New servants are surprised
at it.

Mr. Umewaka Minoru has tried hard not to
change any detail of the old customs. In recent
times many have urged him to change the lights,
but he prefers the old candles. They ask him to
modernize the text and to keep the shite from sitting
in the middle [of the stage ? or of the play ?], but
he won't.

---

[1] This looks like a sort of syncopation. I don't know enough
about music to consider it musically with any fullness, but it
offers to the student of metric most interesting parallels, or if
not parallels, suggestions for comparison with sapphics and with
some of the troubadour measures (notably those of Arnaut
Daniel), the chief trouble being that Professor Fenollosa's notes
at this point are not absolutely lucid.

SUMA GENJI

A pupil of his, a wood-dealer, says that a proper Noh stage could not be built now, for it is all of hinoten. The floor is in twenty pieces, each of which would now cost 250 yen. There must be no knots in the pillars, and all the large pillars and cross pieces are of one piece. This would cost enormously now even if it were possible at all.

Awoyama Shimotsuke no Kami Roju built this stage [the one now used by Minoru] for his villa in Aoyama more than forty years ago; it was moved to its present site in the fourth year of Meiji (1872). The daimyo sold it to a curio dealer from whom Umewaka Minoru bought it. Shimotsuke was some relation to the daimyo of Bishu, in Owari, and so he got the timbers for nothing. The best timber comes from Owari. So the stage had cost only the carpenter's wages (2000 yen?). Now the wood alone would cost 20,000 to 40,000 yen, if you could get it at all. You couldn't contract for it.

The form of the stage was fixed in the time of Hideyoshi and Iyeyasu. In Ashikaga (fourteenth century) the performances were in Tadasu ga wara, and the stage was open on all sides. The bridge came to the middle of one side (apparently the back) where the pine tree now is. The stage was square, as it now is, with four pillars. The audience surrounded it in a great circle " like Sumo " [whatever that may mean]. They had a second story or gallery and the Shogun sat in front. The roof was as it now is.

' NOH '

The roof should not be tiled, but should be like the roof of the shinto temples in Ise. Shimotsuke had had a tiled roof because he was afraid of fire. People had said that he (Minoru) was mad to set up a Noh stage [at the time when he was starting to revive the performance] ; so he had made the roof small and inconspicuous to attract less notice.

Under the stage are set five earthen jars, in the space bounded by the pillars, to make the sound reverberate—both the singing and the stamping.[1] There are two more jars under the musicians' place and three under the bridge. This has been so since early Tokugawa times. The ground is hollowed out under the stage to the depth of four feet.[2]

The jars are not set upright, as this would obstruct the sound. They are set at 45 degrees. Sometimes they are hung by strings and sometimes set on posts. Minoru's are on posts.

Some jars are faced right and some left ; there is a middle one upright. Minoru says it is just like a drum, and that the curve of the jars has to be carefully made. The larger the jars the better.

Hideyoshi or Iyeyasu put the back on the stage. It is made of a double set of boards in order to throw the sound forward. They didn't like having the sound wasted. This innovation was, on that score, aesthetic.

---

[1] This stamping dates from the time when some mythological person danced on a tub to attract the light-goddess.

[2] The stage is in the open. Minoru says elsewhere, " Snow is worst for it blows on the stage and gets on the feet."

SUMA GENJI

" Social and palace " reasons have in some measure determined the form of the stage.

The floor is not quite level, but slopes slightly forward. The art of stage-building is a secret of " daiko." It is as difficult to build a Noh stage as to build a shinto temple, and there are no proper Noh stages built now.

The painting of the pine tree on the back is most important. It is a congratulatory symbol of unchanging green and strength.

On some stages they have small plum flowers, but this is incorrect ; there should be no colour except the green. The bamboo is the complement of the pine. To paint these trees well is a great secret of Kano artists. When skilfully painted, they set off the musicians' forms.

The three real little pine trees along the bridge are quite fixed ; they symbolize heaven, earth, and man. The one for heaven is nearest the stage, and then comes the one which symbolizes man. They are merely symbols like the painted pine tree. Sometimes when a pine is mentioned the actors look toward it.

The measurements of the stage have not changed since early Tokugawa days. It should be three ken square, but this measurement is sometimes taken inside, sometimes outside the pillars.

There is no special symbolism in the bridge ; it is merely a way of getting across. The length was arbitrary under the Ashikaga ; later it was fixed by rule. At the Shogun's court the bridge was 13 ken long, and one needed a great voice to act there. The middle palace bridge was 7 ken. Minoru's bridge is 5 ken. The bridge must be an odd number of ken, like 13, or like the " in " and " yo " numbers (7 and 5). The width is 9 " shaken " outside and 8 inside the pillars.

PART II

THE reader, having perused thus far in patience or in impatience, will probably want to know what came of it all. Does the present Noh, saved from the ashes of the revolution, justify so minute an examination of its past? Believing, as I do, that the Noh is a very great art, I can heartily say that it does. I give here several further specimens of the text or libretto. The reader must remember that the words are only one part of this art. The words are fused with the music and with the ceremonial dancing. One must read or " examine " these texts " as if one were listening to music." One must build out of their indefiniteness a definite image. The plays are at their best, I think, an image ; that is to say, their unity lies in the image—they are built up about it as the Greek plays are built up about a single moral conviction. The Greek plays are elaborate presentations of some incident of a story well known ; so also the Japanese plays rely upon a certain knowledge of past story or legend.

They present some more vivid hour or crisis. The Greek plays are troubled and solved by the gods ; the Japanese are abounding in ghosts and spirits. Often the spirit appears first in some homely guise, as, in Catholic legend, we find Christ appearing as a beggar.

The spirit seems often an old man or old woman rapt in meditation. In Kumasaka we come upon a simple recluse. The plot is as follows :

The pilgrim priest is asked to pray for some anonymous soul. His interlocutor's hut has in it no shrine, no single picture of Buddha, nothing but a spear and an iron mace. The owner of the hut alludes to himself as " this priest." His gospel is the very simple one of protecting travellers from neighbouring bandits.

Suddenly both he and his hut disappear (vide the comments of the chorus). The pilgrim, however, having begun his prayer for the unknown dead man, goes on with the service.

He is rewarded. The second act opens with the reappearance of the spirit in splendid array. He is the spirit of Kumasaka, remembering the glory of his days, meditating upon them, upon his bowmen and deeds of arms. The final passage is the Homeric presentation of combat between him and the young boy, Ushiwaka. But note here the punctilio. Kumasaka's spirit returns to do justice to the glory of Ushiwaka and to tell of his own defeat. All this is symbolized in the dance climax of the play, and is told out by the chorus.

KUMASAKA

A Play in two Acts, by Ujinobu, adopted son of Motokiyo

CHARACTERS

A PRIEST.

FIRST SHITE, or HERO, the apparition of KUMASAKA in the form of an old priest.

SECOND SHITE, the apparition of KUMASAKA in his true form.

CHORUS. This chorus sometimes speaks what the chief characters are thinking, sometimes it describes or interprets the meaning of their movements.

PLOT.—The ghost of Kumasaka makes reparation for his brigandage by protecting the country. He comes back to praise the bravery of the young man who had killed him in single combat.

PRIEST

Where shall I rest, wandering weary of the world ? I am a city-bred priest, I have not

67

seen the east counties, and I've a mind to go there. Crossing the hills, I look on the lake of Omi, on the woods of Awatsu. Going over the long bridge at Seta, I rested a night at Noji, and another at Shinohara, and at the dawn I came to the green field, Awono in Miwo. I now pass Akasaka at sunset.

SHITE

(in the form of an old priest)

I could tell that priest a thing or two.

PRIEST

Do you mean me ? What is it ?

SHITE

A certain man died on this day. I ask you to pray for him.

PRIEST

All right; but whom shall I pray for ?

SHITE

I will not tell you his name, but his grave lies in the green field beyond that tall pine tree. He cannot enter the gates of Paradise, and so I ask you to pray.

KUMASAKA

Priest

But I do not think it is right for me to pray unless you tell me his name.

Shite

No, no ; you can pray the prayer, Ho kai shujo biodo ri aku ; that would do.

Priest
(praying)

Unto all mortals let there be equal grace, to pass from this life of agony by the gates of death into law ; into the peaceful kingdom.

Shite
(saying first a word or two)

If you pray for him,——

Chorus
(continuing the sentence)

—If you pray with the prayer of " Exeat " he will be thankful, and you need not then know his name. They say that prayer can be heard for even the grass and the plants, for even the sand and the soil here ; and they will surely hear it, if you pray for an unknown man.

'NOH'

SHITE

Will you come in ? This is my cottage.

PRIEST

This is your house ? Very well, I will hold
the service in your house ; but I see no picture
of Buddha nor any wooden image in this
cottage—nothing but a long spear on one wall
and an iron stick in place of a priest's wand,
and many arrows. What are these for ?

SHITE
(*thinking*)

Yes, this priest is still in the first stage of
faith. (*Aloud.*) As you see, there are many
villages here : Tarui, Awohaka, and Akasaka.
But the tall grass of Awo-no-gahara grows
round the roads between them, and the forest
is thick at Koyasu and Awohaka, and many
robbers come out under the rains. They
attack the baggage on horseback, and take the
clothing of maids and servants who pass here.
So I go out with his spear.

PRIEST

That's very fine, isn't it ?

KUMASAKA

Chorus

You will think it very strange for a priest to do this, but even Buddha has the sharp sword of Mida, and Aizen Miowo has arrows, and Tamon, taking his long spear, throws down the evil spirits.

Shite

The deep love——

Chorus

——is excellent. Good feeling and keeping order are much more excellent than the love of Bosatsu. "I think of these matters and know little of anything else. It is from my own heart that I am lost, wandering. But if I begin talking I shall keep on talking until dawn. Go to bed, good father, I will sleep too."

He seemed to be going to his bedroom, but suddenly his figure disappeared, and the cottage became a field of grass. The priest passes the night under the pine trees.

Priest

I cannot sleep out the night. Perhaps if I held my service during the night under this pine tree——

[*He begins his service for the dead man.*

'NOH'

PART SECOND

Second Shite

There are winds in the east and south ; the clouds are not calm in the west ; and in the north the wind of the dark evening blusters ; and under the shade of the mountain——

Chorus

——there is a rustling of boughs and leaves.

Second Shite

Perhaps there will be moonshine to-night, but the clouds veil the sky ; the moon will not break up their shadow. " Have at them ! " " Ho, there ! " " Dash in ! " That is the way I would shout, calling and ordering my men before and behind, my bowmen and horsemen. I plundered men of their treasure, that was my work in the world, and now I must go on ; it is sorry work for a spirit.

Priest

Are you Kumasaka Chohan ? Tell me the tale of your years.

72

KUMASAKA

Second Shite
(*now known as* Kumasaka)

There were great merchants in Sanjo, Yo-shitsugu, and Nobutaka ; they collected treasure each year ; they sent rich goods up to Oku. It was then I assailed their trains. Would you know what men were with me ?

Priest

Tell me the chief men ; were they from many a province ?

Kumasaka

There was Kakusho of Kawachi, there were the two brothers Suriharitaro ; they have no rivals in fencing.[1]

Priest

What chiefs came to you from the city ?

Kumasaka

Emon of Sanjo, Kozari of Mibu.

Priest

In the fighting with torches and in mêlée——

[1] "Omoteuchi," face-to-face attack.

73

KUMASAKA

—they had no equals.

PRIEST

In northern Hakoku ?

KUMASAKA

Were Aso no Matsuwaka and Mikune no Kuro.

PRIEST

In Kaga ?

KUMASAKA

No, Chohan was the head there. There were seventy comrades who were very strong and skilful.

CHORUS

While Yoshitsugu was going along in the fields and on the mountains, we set many spies to take him.

KUMASAKA

Let us say that he is come to the village of Akasaka. This is the best place to attack him. There are many ways to escape if we are defeated, and he has invited many guests and has had a great feast at the inn.

KUMASAKA

Priest

When the night was advanced the brothers Yoshitsugu and Nobutaka fell asleep.

Kumasaka

But there was a small boy with keen eyes, about sixteen or seventeen years old, and he was looking through a little hole in the partition, alert to the slightest noise.

Priest

He did not sleep even a wink.

Kumasaka

We did not know it was Ushiwaka.

Priest

It was fate.

Kumasaka

The hour had come.

Priest

Be quick !

Kumasaka

Have at them !

75

Chorus

(describing the original combat, now symbolized in the dance)

At this word they rushed in, one after another. They seized the torches ; it seemed as if gods could not face them. Ushiwaka stood unafraid ; he seized a small halberd and fought like a lion in earnest, like a tiger rushing, like a bird swooping. He fought so cleverly that he felled the thirteen who opposed him ; many were wounded besides. They fled without swords or arrows. Then Kumasaka said, " Are you the devil ? Is it a god who has struck down these men with such ease ? Perhaps you are not a man. However, dead men take no plunder, and I'd rather leave this truck of Yoshitsugu's than my corpse." So he took his long spear and was about to make off——

Kumasaka

—But Kumasaka thought——

Chorus

(taking it up)

—What can he do, that young chap, if I ply my secret arts freely ? Be he god or devil, I will grasp him and grind him. I will offer

his body as sacrifice to those whom he has
slain. So he drew back, and holding his long
spear against his side, he hid himself behind
the door and stared at the young lad. Ushiwaka beheld him, and holding his bill at his
side, he crouched at a little distance. Kumasaka
waited likewise. They both waited, alertly ;
then Kumasaka stepped forth swiftly with his
left foot, and struck out with the long spear.
It would have run through an iron wall.
Ushiwaka parried it lightly, swept it away,
left volted. Kumasaka followed and again
lunged out with the spear, and Ushiwaka
parried the spear-blade quite lightly. Then
Kumasaka turned the edge of his spear-blade
towards Ushiwaka and slashed at him, and
Ushiwaka leaped to the right. Kumasaka
lifted his spear and the two weapons were
twisted together. Ushiwaka drew back his
blade. Kumasaka swung with his spear. Ushiwaka led up and stepped in shadow.

Kumasaka tried to find him, and Ushiwaka
slit through the back-chink of his armour ;
this seemed the end of his course, and he was
wroth to be slain by such a young boy.

KUMASAKA

Slowly the wound——

77

'NOH'

Chorus

—seemed to pierce ; his heart failed ; weakness o'ercame him.

Kumasaka

At the foot of this pine tree——

Chorus

—he vanished like a dew.

And so saying, he disappeared among the shades of the pine tree at Akasaka, and night fell.

THE END

SHOJO

THIS little dance-plan or eclogue is, evidently, one of the " opening or closing pieces in praise of the gods or the reign." It is merely a little service of praise to the wine - spirit. It is quite easy to understand, from such a performance as this, why one meets travellers who say, " Noh ? I've seen Noh Dances ; I know nothing about Noh Plays."

WAKI

I am a man called Kofu in a village by Yosu,[1] which is at the foot of Kane Kinzan in China, and because of my filial deference I dreamed a strange dream. And the dream told me that if I would sell saké in the street by Yosu I should be rich. I obeyed. Time passed. I am rich. And this is the strange thing about it : whenever I go to the market, there's the same man comes to drink saké. No matter how much he drinks, his face shows

[1] Yosu, i.e. Yang-tze.

no change. It is curious. When I asked his name, he said, "Shojo." A shojo is a monkey. I waited for him where the river runs out at Jinyo, clipping chrysanthemum petals into the saké. I waited for him before moon-rise.

CHORUS

This is chrysanthemum water. Give me the cup. I take it and look at a friend.

HERO

O saké !

CHORUS

Saké is a word well in season. Saké is best in autumn.

HERO

Though autumn winds blow——

CHORUS

—I am not cold at all.

HERO

I will put cotton over——

CHORUS

—the white chrysanthemum flowers

To keep in the smell.
Now we'll take saké.

SHOJO

Hero

The guests will also see——

Chorus

—the moon and the stars hung out.

Hero

This place is by Jinyo.

Chorus

The feast is on the river.

Hero
(who is in reality Shojo)

Shojo will dance now.

Chorus

The thin leaves of ashi, the leaves of the river reeds, are like flute-notes. The waves are like little drums.

Hero

The voice sounds clear through the shore-winds.

Chorus

It is the sound of autumn.

'NOH'

Hero

You are welcome. I have made this jar full of saké. Take it. It will never run dry.

Chorus

No, it will never be empty—the saké of bamboo leaves ; although you drink from the lasting cup of the autumn, the autumn evening remains ever the same.

The moon fades out of the river, and the saké weighs down my blood.

And I am shaking and falling ; I lie down filled with wine, and I dream ; and, awaking, I find the saké still flowing from the jar of Shojo, from the magical fountain.

THE END

TAMURA

THIS play is to be regarded as one of those dealing with the " pacification of the country and the driving out of evil spirits," although one might perhaps look upon it as a ceremonial play for the Temple founded by Tamura, or even less exactly a ghost play.

The notes are in fragments, or rather there are several long cuts, which do not, however, obscure the outline or structure of the play.

CHARACTERS

HERO, first apparition, a boy (" doji " or temple servant).
TAMURA MARO, second apparition.
WAKI, a priest.

(The opening may be thus summarized : The Waki comes on and says that he is going to Kioto to see the sights. It is spring, and he comes from Kiyomidzu. Sakura are blooming. He wants to ask questions about the place. The boy comes on, describes the flowers, and says that the light of the goddess Kwannon has made them brighter than usual. The Waki asks him who he is " to be standing there in the shade and sweeping up the fallen petals.")

WAKI

Are you the flower-keeper ?

BOY

I am a man who serves the "Jinnushi Gongen." I always sweep in blossom season— so you may call me the flower-keeper, or the honorary servant ; but, whatever name you use, you should think of me as some one of rank, though I am concealed in humble appearance.

WAKI

Yes, you look that. Will you tell me about this temple ?

BOY

This temple is called Seisuiji ; it was founded by Tamura Maro. In Kojimadera of Yamato there was a priest named Kenshin. He was always wishing to see the true light of Kwannon. And one time he saw a golden light floating on the Kotsu River. And he was going toward it, when he met an old man who said to him, " I am Gioye Koji, and you must seek out a certain patron and put up a great temple."

And the old man went off to the East, and he was Kwannon. And the patron was Maro, Sakanouye no Tamura Maro.

Chorus

In this pure water, Kwannon with a thousand hands gives blessing. She blesses this land and this people.

Waki

Well, I have met some one interesting. Can you tell me of other places about here ?

Boy

The peak to the south is Nakayama Sei-kanji.

Waki

And what is that temple to the northward where they are ringing the nightfall bell ?

Boy

That is the temple of Ashino-o. Look ! the moon is lifting itself over Mount Otoba,[1] and lights the cherry flowers. You must look !

[1] Otoba, " sounding-wings."

'NOH'

Waki

It is an hour outweighing much silver.
[*The* Boy *and the* Priest *together recite the Chinese poem.*

One moment of this spring night is worth a full thousand gold bars.
The flowers have a fine smell under the moon.[1]

[*There is a break here in the notes. There should follow a chorus about cherries under the moon.*

Chorus

Having seen these things with you, I know you are out of the common. I wonder what your name is.

Boy

If you want to discover my name, you must watch what road I take. You must see to what I return.

Chorus

We cannot know the far or near of his route.

Boy

I go into the mountains.

---

[1] Two lines from a poem by the Chinese poet Su Shih, A.D. 1036–1101.

TAMURA

Chorus

He said : " Watch my path." And he went down in front of the Jinnushi Gongen temple, and to Tamura-do. He opened the door and went in.

END OF PART ONE

II

Waki

I have watched all night under the cherries. I do service beneath the full moon.

[*He performs a service.*

Hero

(*in his second apparition, no longer the boy, but* Tamura Maro)

That is a very blessed scripture. Just because you have droned it over, I am able to come here and speak with the traveller. This is the blessing of Kwannon.

Waki

How strange ! A man appears, lit up by the light of the flowers. What are you ?

87

'NOH'

TAMURA

To be open, I am none other than Saka-no-Uye Tamura Maro, out of the time of Heijo Tenno. I conquered the eastern wild men, beat down their evil spirit, and was an honest servant to my Emperor by the grace of this temple's Buddha.

[*Here there follows a passage in which he describes his battles.*

CHORUS

The Emperor bade me beat down the evil spirits in Suzuka in Ise, and to set the capital of that country in peace. I drew up my forces, and then, before I set out, I came to this Kwannon and prayed.

TAMURA

And then a strange sign appeared.

CHORUS

Having faith in the true smile of Kwannon, he went swiftly to war, out past Osaka to the forest Awadzu. He passed Ishiyamaji, and, thinking it one of the gods of Kiyomidzu, he prayed on the long bridge of Seta, as he was come nigh to Ise.

TAMURA

(*changing from narrative of the journey
to description*)

There the plum-trees were blossoming.   All
the scene showed the favour of Kwannon and
the virtue of the Emperor.

Then there was a great noise of evil voices,
a shaking of mountains.

TAMURA
(*excitedly, and as if amid the original scene*)

Hear ye the evil spirits !   Once in the reign
of Tenshi, the evil spirit who served the bad
minister Chikata died, and Chikata fell.   But
you are near to Suzukayama ;   you are easy
to kill.

CHORUS

Look to the sea of Ise, on the pine-moor
of Anono the evil spirits rain their black clouds.
They pour down fires of iron ;   they move
like ten thousand footmen ;   they are piled
like the mountains.

TAMURA

Look forth on the carnage !

'NOH'

Chorus

The battle ! Senju Kwannon pours lights on our banner. Her lights fly about in the air. She holds in her thousand hands the bow of " Great Mercy." Hers are the arrows of wisdom. Fly forth her thousand arrows. They harry the spirits ; they fall in a swirl of hail. The spirits are dead from her rain.

How Great is the Mercy of Kwannon ! [1]

[1] Tamura Maro had a special devotion to the Kwannon of the Seisui Temple. Her image, thousand-handed with an arrow in each hand, was woven on his battle-banners.

THE END

FOREWORD TO TSUNEMASA

THE Noh, especially the Noh of spirits, abounds in dramatic situations, perhaps too subtle and fragile for our western stage, but none the less intensely dramatic. Kumasaka is martial despite the touch of Buddhism in the opening scene, where the spirit is atoning for his past violence.

Tsunemasa is gentle and melancholy. It is all at high tension, but it is a psychological tension, the tension of the séance. The excitement and triumph are the nervous excitement and triumph of a successful ritual. The spirit is invoked and appears.

The parallels with Western spiritist doctrines are more than interesting. Note the spirit's uncertainty as to his own success in appearing. The priest wonders if he really saw anything. The spirit affirms that " The body was there if you saw it."

As to the quality of poetry in this work : there is the favoured youth, soon slain ; the

uneasy blood-stained and thoughtless spirit ;
there are the lines about the caged stork crying
at sunset, and they are as clear as Dante's.

" Era già l' ora che volge il disio."

TSUNEMASA

PRIEST

I AM Sodzu Giokei, keeper of the temple of
Ninnaji. Tajima no Kami Tsunemasa, of the
house of Taira, was loved by the Emperor
when he was a boy, but he was killed in the
old days at the battle of the West Seas. And
this is the Seizan lute that the Emperor gave
him before that fighting. I offer this lute to
his spirit in place of libation ; I do the right
service before him.

[*They perform a service to the spirit of
Tsunemasa.*

PRIEST

Although it is midnight I see the form of
a man, a faint form, in the light there. If
you are spirit, who are you ?

SPIRIT

I am the ghost of Tsunemasa. Your service
has brought me.

TSUNEMASA

Priest

Is it the ghost of Tsunemasa? I perceive no form, but a voice.

Spirit

It is the faint sound alone that remains.

Priest

O! But I saw the form, really.

Spirit

It is there if you see it.

Priest

I can see.

Spirit

Are you sure that you see it, really?

Priest

O, do I, or do I not see you?

Chorus

Changeful Tsunemasa, full of the universal unstillness, looked back upon the world. His voice was heard there, a voice without form. None might see him, but he looked out from his phantom, a dream that gazed on our world.

93

'NOH'

PRIEST

It is strange! Tsunemasa! The figure was there and is gone, only the thin sound remains. The film of a dream, perhaps! It was a reward for this service.

SPIRIT

When I was young I went into the court. I had a look at life then. I had high favour. I was given the Emperor's biwa.[1] That is the very lute you have there. It is the lute called "Seizan." I had it when I walked through the world.

CHORUS

It is the lute that he had in this world, but now he will play Buddha's music.

PRIEST

Bring out what stringed lutes you possess, and follow his music.

SPIRIT

And I will lead you unseen.

[*He plays.*

[1] Lute.

TSUNEMASA

Priest

Midnight is come ; we will play the " midnight-play," Yabanraku.

Spirit

The clear sky is become overclouded ; the rain walks with heavier feet.

Priest

They shake the grass and the trees.

Spirit

It was not the rain's feet. Look yonder.

Chorus

A moon hangs clear on the pine-bough. The wind rustles as if flurried with rain. It is an hour of magic. The bass strings are something like rain ; the small strings talk like a whisper. The deep string is a wind voice of autumn ; the third and the fourth strings are like the crying stork in her cage, when she thinks of her young birds toward nightfall. Let the cocks leave off their crowing. Let no one announce the dawn.

'NOH'

SPIRIT

A flute's voice has moved the clouds of Shushinrei. And the phœnix come out from the cloud; they descend with their playing. Pitiful, marvellous music! I have come down to the world. I have resumed my old playing. And I was happy here. All that is soon over.

PRIEST

Now I can see him again, the figure I saw here; can it be Tsunemasa?

SPIRIT

It's a sorry face that I make here. Put down the lights if you see me.

CHORUS

The sorrow of the heart is a spreading around of quick fires. The flames are turned to thick rain. He slew by the sword and was slain. The red wave of blood rose in fire, and now he burns with that flame. He bade us put out the lights; he flew as a summer moth.

> His brushing wings were a storm.
> His spirit is gone in the darkness.

FINIS

PART III

FENOLLOSA ON THE NOH

THE Japanese people have loved nature so passionately that they have interwoven her life and their own into one continuous drama of the art of pure living. I have written elsewhere [1] of the five Acts into which this life-drama falls, particularly as it reveals itself in the several forms of their visual arts. I have spoken of the universal value of this special art-life, and explained how the inflowing of such an Oriental stream has helped to revitalize Western Art, and must go on to assist in the solution of our practical educational problems. I would now go back to that other key, to the blossoming of Japanese genius, which I mentioned under my account of the flower festivals, namely, the national poetry, and its rise, through the enriching of four successive periods, to a vital dramatic force in the fifteenth century.

[1] "Epochs of Chinese and Japanese Art," by Ernest Fenollosa. London : Heinemann, 1911.

99

Surely literature may be as delicate an exponent
of a nation's soul as is art ; and there are several
phases of Oriental poetry, both Japanese and
Chinese, which have practical significance and
even inspiration for us in this weak, transitional
period of our Western poetic life.

We cannot escape, in the coming centuries,
even if we would, a stronger and stronger
modification of our established standards by
the pungent subtlety of Oriental thought,
and the power of the condensed Oriental forms.
The value will lie partly in relief from the
deadening boundaries of our own conventions.
This is no new thing. It can be shown that
the freedom of the Elizabethan mind, and its
power to range over all planes of human
experience, as in Shakespeare, was, in part, an
aftermath of Oriental contacts—in the Crusades,
in an intimacy with the Mongols such as Marco
Polo's, in the discovery of a double sea-passage
to Persia and India, and in the first gleanings
of the Jesuit missions to Asia. Still more
clearly can it be shown that the romantic movement in English poetry, in the later eighteenth
century and the early nineteenth, was influenced and enriched, though often in a subtle
and hidden way, by the beginnings of scholarly
study and translation of Oriental literature.

FENOLLOSA ON THE NOH

Bishop Percy, who afterwards revived our knowledge of the mediaeval ballad, published early in the 1760's the first appreciative English account of Chinese poetry ; and Bishop Hood wrote an essay on the Chinese theatre, seriously comparing it with the Greek. A few years later Voltaire published his first Chinese tragedy, modified from a Jesuit translation ; and an independent English version held the London stage till 1824. Moore, Byron, Shelley, and Coleridge were influenced by the spirit, and often by the very subject, of Persian translations ; and Wordsworth's " Intimations of Immortality " verges on the Hindoo doctrine of reincarnation. In these later days India powerfully reacts upon our imagination through an increasingly intimate knowledge. . . .

I

A form of drama, as primitive, as intense, and almost as beautiful as the ancient Greek drama at Athens, still exists in the world. Yet few care for it, or see it.[1] In the fifth century before Christ the Greek drama arose out of the religious rites practised in the festivals of the God of Wine. In the fifteenth century

[1] The Noh has been "popularized" since Fenollosa wrote this.

after Christ, the Japanese drama arose out of religious rites practised in the festivals of the Shinto gods, chiefly the Shinto god of the Kasuga temple at Nara. Both began by a sacred dance, and both added a sacred chorus sung by priests. The transition from a dance chorus to drama proper consisted, in both cases, in the evolving of a solo part, the words of which alternate in dialogue with the chorus. In both the final form of drama consists of a few short scenes, wherein two or three soloists act a main theme, whose deeper meaning is interpreted by the poetical comment of the chorus. In both the speech was metrical, and involved a clear organic structure of separate lyrical units. In both music played an important part. In both action was a modification of the dance. In both rich costumes were worn ; in both, masks. The form and tradition of the Athenian drama passed over into the tradition of the ancient Roman stage, and died away in the early middle ages fourteen centuries ago. It is dead, and we can study it from scant records only. But the Japanese poetic drama is alive to-day, having been transmitted almost unchanged from one perfected form reached in Kioto in the fifteenth century.

FENOLLOSA ON THE NOH

It has been said that all later drama has been influenced by the Greek ; that the strolling jugglers and contortionists, who wandered in troupes over Europe in the middle ages, constitute an unbroken link between the degenerate Roman actors and the miracle plays of the church, which grew into the Shakespearean drama. It is even asserted that, as the Greek conquest gave rise to a Greco-Buddhist form of sculpture on the borders of India and China, Greek dramatic influence entered also into the Hindoo and Chinese drama, and eventually into the Noh of Japan. But the effect of foreign thought on the Noh is small in comparison with that of the native Shinto influences. It is as absurd to say that the Noh is an offshoot of Greek drama as it would be to say that Shakespeare is such an offshoot.

There is, however, beside the deeper analogy of the Japanese Noh with Greek plays, an interesting secondary analogy with the origin of Shakespeare's art. All three had an independent growth from miracle plays—the first from the plays of the worship of Bacchus, the second from the plays of the worship of Christ, the third from the plays of the worship of the Shinto deities and of Buddha. The plays that preceded Shakespeare's in England

were acted in fields adjoining the churches,
and later in the courtyards of nobles. The
plays that preceded the Noh, and even the
Noh themselves, were enacted, first in the
gardens of temples or on the dry river-beds
adjoining the temples, and later in the courtyards of the daimio. On the other hand, the
actual modus of the Shakespearean drama is
practically dead for us. Occasional revivals
have to borrow scenery and other contrivances
unknown to the Elizabethan stage, and the
continuity of professional tradition has certainly been broken. But in the Japanese Noh,
though it arose one hundred years before
Shakespeare, this continuity has never been
broken. The same plays are to-day enacted
in the same manner as then ; even the leading
actors of to-day are blood descendants of the
very men who created this drama 450 years
ago.

This ancient lyric drama is not to be
confounded with the modern realistic drama
of Tokio, with such drama, for instance, as
Danjuro's. This vulgar drama is quite like
ours, with an elaborate stage and scenery, with
little music or chorus, and no masks ; with
nothing, in short, but realism and mimetics
of action. This modern drama, a ghost of the

fifth period, arose in Yedo some 300 years ago. It was an amusement designed by the common people for themselves, and was written and acted by them. It therefore corresponds to the work of Ukiyo-ye in painting, and more especially to the colour prints ; and a large number of these prints reproduce characters and scenes from the people's theatre.

As the pictorial art of the fifth period was divisible into two parts—that of the nobility, designed to adorn their castles, and that of the common people, printed illustration,—so has the drama of the last 200 years been twofold, that of the lyric Noh, preserved pure in the palaces of the rich ; and that of the populace, running to realism and extravagance in the street theatres. To-day, in spite of the shock and revolution of 1868, the former, the severe and poetic drama, has been revived, and is enthusiastically studied by cultured Japanese. In that commotion the palaces of the daimios, with their Noh stages, were destroyed, the court troupes of actors were dispersed. For three years after 1868 performances ceased entirely. But Mr. Umewaka Minoru, who had been one of the soloists in the Shogun's central troupe, kept guard over the pure tradition, and had many stage directions or

" tenets " preserved in writing along with the texts. In 1871 he bought an ex-daimio's stage for a song, set it up on the banks of the Sumida river in Tokio, and began to train his sons. Many patient pupils and old actors flocked to him ; the public began their patronage ; he bought up collections of costumes and masks at sales of impoverished nobles ; and now his theatre is so thronged that boxes have to be engaged a week beforehand, and five other theatres have been built in Tokio. . . .

For the last twenty years I have been studying the Noh, under the personal tuition of Umewaka Minoru and his sons, learning by actual practice the method of the singing and something of the acting ; I have taken down from Umewaka's lips invaluable oral traditions of the stage as it was before 1868 ; and have prepared, with his assistance and that of native scholars, translations of some fifty of the texts.

II

The art of dance has played a richer part in Chinese and Japanese life than it has in Europe. In prehistoric days, when men or women were strongly moved, they got up and danced. It was as natural a form of self-expression as improvised verse or song, and

was often combined with both. But the growing decorum of a polite society tended to
relegate this dancing to occasions of special
inspiration and to professional dancers. These
occasions were roughly of two sorts—formal
entertainments at Court and religious ceremonial. The former, which survives to this
day in the Mikado's palace, represented the
action of historic heroes, frequently warriors
posturing with sword and spear. This was
accompanied by the instrumental music of a
full orchestra. The religious ceremonial was
of two sorts—the Buddhist miracle plays in
the early temples and the god dances of the
Shinto.

The miracle plays represented scenes from
the lives of saints and the intervention of Buddha
and Bodhisattwa in human affairs. Like the
very earliest forms of the European play,
these were pantomimic, with no special dramatic
text, save possibly the reading of appropriate
scripture. The Japanese miracle plays were
danced with masks ; and the temples of Nara
are still full of these masks, which date from
the eighth century. It is clear that many
popular and humorous types must have been
represented ; and it is barely possible that
these were remotely derived, through Greco-

Buddhist channels, from the masks of Greek low comedy. In these plays the god is the chief actor, sometimes in dramatic relation to a human companion. The god always wears a mask. The solo part is established ; and herein the play differs from the Greek, where the original rite was performed by a group of priests, or (in the comedy) by goats or fauns.

The most certainly Japanese element of the drama was the sacred dance in the Shinto temples. This was a kind of pantomime, and repeated the action of a local god on his first appearance to men. The first dance, therefore, was a god dance ; the god himself danced, with his face concealed in a mask. Here is a difference between the Greek and Japanese beginnings. In Greece the chorus danced, and the god was represented by an altar. In Japan the god danced alone.

The ancient Shinto dance or pantomime was probably, at first, a story enacted by the local spirit, as soloist—a repetition, as it were, of the original manifestation. Shintoism is spiritism, mild, nature-loving, much like the Greek. A local spirit appeared to men in some characteristic phase. On the spot a Shinto temple was built, and yearly or monthly rites, including pantomime, perpetuated the memory of the event. Such things happened all over the country ; and thus thousands of different stories were perpetuated in the dances —hence the wealth of primitive material. The thing can be seen to-day in every village festival. Even in great cities like Tokio, every district maintains its primitive village spirit-worship, that of some tutelary worthy who enacts the old story once a year on a specially made platform raised in the street, about which the people of the locality congregate. The plays are generally pantomime without text.

In the Shinto dance the soloist has no chorus. He performs some religious act of the spirit, though this is often turned into rude comedy. This dance takes the form of a dignified pantomime. It is not an abstract kicking or whirling, not a mere dervish frenzy, but is full of meaning, representing divine situations and emotions, artistically, with restraint and with the chastening of a conventional beauty, which makes every posture of the whole body—head, trunk, hands, and feet —harmonious in line, and all the transitions from posture to posture balanced and graceful in line. A flashlight glimpse across such a dance is like a flashlight of sculpture ; but the motion itself, like a picture which moves in colour, is like the art of music. There is an orchestral accompaniment of flutes, drums, and cymbals, slow, fast, low, passionate, or accented, that makes a natural ground-tone. Akin to these are the moving street pageants, which are like early European pageants, or even those of to-day in Catholic countries.

Thus the three sources of the Noh, all belonging to the first period, are, in the order of their influence, (1) the Shinto god dance, (2) the warrior court dance, (3) the Buddhist sacred pantomime.

As the old Chinese court dances were modified in the aristocratic life of the second period, it was natural that lovers of poetry should begin to add poetical comment to the entertainment. Thus the next step consisted in the addition of a text for a chorus to sing during the solo dance. They were already used to accompany their verses with the lute.

In the first of the five periods, Japanese lyric poetry reached its height. It was quite different from the Chinese, as the language is polysyllabic, the sentences long and smooth, the tone gently contemplative. About the year 900, when the capital had been removed to Kioto, the longer and straggling verse structure went out of fashion. A tense stanzaic form had come into almost universal use. This fashion may be referred to Chinese influence. Rhyme, however, was not introduced. The lines, usually of five or seven syllables, are rich and sonorous. Soon afterwards the passion for composing and reciting this Japanese poetry became so powerful among the educated classes, especially in the cultured aristocracy at Kioto, where men and women met on equal terms, that the old court entertainments of dance and music had to be modified to admit the use of poetic texts. At first the nobles themselves, at their feasts or at court ceremonies, sang in unison songs composed for the occasion. The next step was to write songs appropriate to the dances ; finally the chorus of nobles became a trained chorus, accompanied by court musicians. Thus by the end of the ninth century there was a body of performers definitely associated with the court, with a minister in charge of it. There were two divisions. The composition of the texts and the composition of the music and dances were allotted to different persons. At this stage the old Chinese subjects fell into the background, and subjects of Japanese historical interest, or of more national and lyric nature, were substituted.

Thus arose the court entertainment called
Saibara, which ceased to be practised after the
twelfth century. Most of the details of it are
hopelessly lost, though a few texts remain
from a manuscript collection compiled about
the year 900. The music and dance are
utterly lost, except so far as we can discern a
trace of what they must have been, in the later
practices of the Noh. It is interesting to find
that the very names of some of the pieces in
Saibara are identical with those used in Noh
five centuries later. The Saibara pieces are
very short, much like the lyric poems of the
day ; and they are often so lyrical or so personal as hardly to suggest how they may have
been danced. It is also uncertain whether
these brief texts were repeated over and over,
or at intervals during the long dance, or whether
they were a mere introduction to a dance which
elaborated their thought.[1] The following Saibara will serve as example :

---

[1] Professor Fenollosa, in an earlier half-sentence which I have
omitted, would seem to underestimate the effect of the dance
on European art forms. It was from the May-day dance and
dance - songs that the Provençal poetry probably arose. By
stages came strophe and antistrophe tenzone, the Spanish loa and
entremes. See also W. P. Ker, " English Mediaeval Literature,"
pp. 79 et seq., for the spread of the dance through Europe and the
effect on the lyric forms. Compare also the first Saibara given
in the text with the Provençal " A l'entrada del temps clar."

FENOLLOSA ON THE NOH

O white-gemmed camelia and you jewel willow,
Who stand together on the Cape of Takasago !
This one, since I want her for mine,
That one, too, since I want her for mine—
Jewel willow !
I will make you a thing to hang my cloak on,
With its tied - up strings, with its deep - dyed
    strings.
Ah ! what have I done ?
There, what is this I am doing ?
O what am I to do ?
Mayhap I have lost my soul !
But I have met
The lily flower,
The first flower of morning.

This new combination of dance and song
soon spread from the court ceremonies to the
religious rites of the god dances in the Shinto
temples, not, however, to the Buddhist, which
were too much under the influence of Hindu
and Chinese thought to care for Japanese verse.
In Shinto dances the subject was already pure
Japanese and fit for Japanese texts ; and it
may very well have occurred to some priest, in
one of the thousand Shinto matsuris (festivals)
going on all over the land, to sing a poem concerning the subject of the dance. By the end
of the ninth century, in the second period, this
custom had become common in the great

Shinto festivals, in the Mikado's private chapel,
and at Kasuga. The texts were sung by a
trained chorus, and here is a second difference
from the line of Greek advance. In Greece
the chorus not only sang but danced ; in
Japan the chorus did not dance or act, but
was merely contemplative, sitting at the side.
The songs so sung were called Kagura.

A few examples of these ancient Shinto
texts for Kagura have come down to us.
They are not exactly prayers ; they are often
lovely poems of nature, for, after all, these
Shinto gods were a harmless kind of nature
spirit clinging to grottoes, rivers, trees, and
mountains. It is curious to note that the structure of the texts is always double, like the
Greek strophe and antistrophe. They were
probably sung by a double chorus ; and this
is doubtless the basis of the alternation or
choric dialogue.

Here is a kagura, sung by a priestess to her
wand :

Strophe.   As for this mitegura,
As for this mitegura,
It is not mine at all ;
It is the mitegura of a god,
Called the Princess Toyooka,
Who lives in heaven,

FENOLLOSA ON THE NOH

> The mitegura of a god,
> The mitegura of a god.

Antistrophe. O how I wish in vain that I could
turn myself into a mitegura,
That I might be taken into the hand
of the Mother of the Gods,
That I might come close to the heart
of a god, close to the heart of a
god !

III

We have now come to the point where we
can deal with this mass of playwriting as
literature. The plays are written in a mixture
of prose and verse. The finest parts are in
verse ; ordinary conversation lapses into prose ;
the choruses are always in verse.

It appears that the first period of Japanese
civilization supplied the chance elements for
the Noh, that is, the dances and certain attitudes
of mind. The second period supplied the
beginnings of literary texts. The third period,
dating from the end of the twelfth century, is
marked by the rise of the military classes and
supplied naturally a new range of dramatic
motives. The land was filled with tales of
wild achievement and knight-errantry and
with a passionate love for individuality, how-

ever humble. The old court customs and
dances of the supplanted nobles were kept
up solely in the peaceful enclosures of the
Shinto temples. New forms of entertainment
arose. Buddhism threw away scholarship and
mystery, and aimed only at personal salvation.
As in contemporary Europe, itinerant monks
scoured the country, carrying inspiration from
house to house. Thus arose a semi-epic literature, in which the deeds of martial heroes were
gathered into several great cycles of legend,
like the Carolingian and the Arthurian cycles
in Europe. Such were the Heike epic, the
Soga cycle, and a dozen others. Episodes
from these were sung by individual minstrels
to the accompaniment of a lute. One of the
most important effects of this new epic balladry
was to widen greatly the scope of motives
acceptable for plays.

As for comedy, another movement was
growing up in the country, from farmers'
festivals, the spring sowing of the rice, and the
autumn reaping. These were at first mere
buffooneries or gymnastic contests arranged
by the villagers for their amusement. They
were called Dengaku, a rice-field music. Later,
professional troupes of Dengaku jugglers and
acrobats were kept by the daimios in their

palaces, and eventually by the authorities of the Buddhist and Shinto temples, in order to attract crowds to their periodic festivals. Such professional troupes began to add rude country farces to their stock of entertainments, at first bits of coarse impromptu repartee, consisting of tricks by rustics upon each other, which were probably not out of harmony with some of the more grotesque and comic Shinto dances. About the twelfth and thirteenth centuries these two elements of comedy—the rustic and the sacred—combined at the Shinto temples, and actors were trained as a permanent troupe. Such farces are called Kiogen. In the later part of the fourteenth century, towards the end, that is, of the third period, Dengaku troupes of Shinto dancers advanced to the incorporating of more tragic subjects, selected from the episodes of the balladry. The god dancer now became, sometimes, a human being, the hero of a dramatic crisis—sometimes even a woman, interchanging dialogue with the chorus, as the two ancient Shinto choruses had sung dialogue in the Kagura.

It was not till the fourth period of Japanese culture, that is to say, early in the fifteenth century, when a new Buddhist civilization, based upon contemplative and poetic insight into nature had arisen, that the inchoate Japanese drama, fostered in the Shinto temples, could take on a moral purpose and a psychologic breadth that should expand it into a vital drama of character. The Shinto god dance, the lyric form of court poetry, the country farces, and a full range of epic incident, in short, all that was best in the earlier Japanese tradition, was gathered into this new form, arranged and purified.

The change came about in this way. The Zen parish priests summoned up to Kioto the Dengaku troupe from Nara, and made it play before the Shogun. The head actor of this Nara troupe, Kwan, took the new solo parts, and greatly enlarged the scope of the music of the other acting. During the lifetime of his son and grandson, Zei and On, hundreds of new plays were created. It is a question to what extent these three men, Kwan, Zei, and On, were the originators of the texts of these new dramas, and how far the Zen priests are responsible. The lives of the former are even more obscure than is Shakespeare's. No full account exists of their work. We have only stray passages from contemporary note-books relating to the great excitement caused by their irregular performances. A great temporary circus was erected on the dry bed of the Kamo river, with its storeys divided into boxes for each noble family, from the Emperor and the Shogun downwards. Great priests managed the show, and used the funds collected for building temples. The stage was a raised open circle in the centre, reached by a long bridge from a dressing-room outside the circus.

We can now see why, even in the full lyric drama, the god dance remains the central feature. All the slow and beautiful postures of the early dramatic portion invariably lead up to the climax of the hero's dance (just as the Greek had planned for the choric dances). This often comes only at the end of the second act, but sometimes also in the first. Most plays have two acts. During the closing dance the chorus sings its finest passages, though it will have been already engaged many times in dialogue with the soloist. Its function is poetical comment, and it carries the mind beyond what the action exhibits to the core of the spiritual meaning. The music is simple melody, hardly more than a chant, accompanied by drums and flutes. There is thus a delicate adjustment of half a dozen conventions appealing to eye, ear, or mind, which produces an intensity of feeling such as belongs to no merely realistic drama. The audience sits spellbound before the tragedy, bathed in tears ; but the effect is never one of realistic horror, rather of a purified and elevated passion, which sees divine purpose under all violence.

The beauty and power of Noh lie in the concentration. All elements—costume, motion, verse, and music—unite to produce a single clarified impression. Each drama embodies some primary human relation or emotion ; and the poetic sweetness or poignancy of this is carried to its highest degree by carefully excluding all such obtrusive elements as a mimetic realism or vulgar sensation might demand. The emotion is always fixed upon idea, not upon personality. The solo parts express great types of human character, derived from Japanese history. Now it is brotherly love, now love to a parent, now loyalty to a master, love of husband and wife, of mother for a dead child, or of jealousy or anger, of self-mastery in battle, of the battle passion itself, of the clinging of a ghost to the scene of its sin, of the infinite compassion of a Buddha, of the sorrow of unrequited love. Some one of these intense emotions is chosen for a piece, and, in it, elevated to the plane of universality by the intensity and purity of treatment. Thus

the drama became a storehouse of history, and
a great moral force for the whole social order
of the Samurai.

After all, the most striking thing about
these plays is their marvellously complete
grasp of spiritual being. They deal more with
heroes, or even we might say ghosts, than with
men clothed in the flesh. Their creators were
great psychologists. In no other drama does
the supernatural play so great, so intimate a
part. The types of ghosts are shown to us;
we see great characters operating under the
conditions of the spirit-life; we observe what
forces have changed them. Bodhisattwa, devas,
elementals, animal spirits, hungry spirits or
pseta, cunning or malicious or angry devils,
dragon kings from the water world, spirits of
the moonlight, the souls of flowers and trees,
essences that live in wine and fire, the semi-
embodiments of a thought—all these come
and move before us in the dramatic types.

These types of character are rendered
particularly vivid to us by the sculptured
masks. Spirits, women, and old men wear
masks; other human beings do not. For the
200 plays now extant, nearly 300 separate
masks are necessary in a complete list of properties. Such variety is far in excess of the

Greek types, and immense vitality is given to a good mask by a great actor, who acts up to it until the very mask seems alive and displays a dozen turns of emotion. The costumes are less carefully individualized. For the hero parts, especially for spirits, they are very rich, of splendid gold brocades and soft floss-silk weaving, or of Chinese tapestry stitch, and are very costly. In Tokugawa days (1602–1868) every rich daimio had his own stage, and his complete collection of properties. The dancing is wonderful—a succession of beautiful poses which make a rich music of line. The whole body acts together, but with dignity. Great play is given to the sleeve, which is often tossed back and forth or raised above the head. The fan also plays a great part, serving for cup, paper, pen, sword, and a dozen other imaginary stage properties. The discipline of the actor is a moral one. He is trained to revere his profession, to make it a sacred act thus to impersonate a hero. He yields himself up to possession by the character. He acts as if he knew himself to be a god, and after the performance he is generally quite exhausted.

FENOLLOSA ON THE NOH

In Dojoji a girl is in love with a priest, who
flees from her and takes shelter under a great
bronze temple bell, which falls over him. Her
sheer force of desire turns her into a dragon,
she bites the top of the bell, twists herself
about the bell seven times, spits flame from
her mouth, and lashes the bronze with her tail.
Then the bell melts away under her, and the
priest she loves dies in the molten mass. In
Kumasaka the boy-warrior, Ushiwaka, fights a
band of fifteen giant robbers in the dark.
They fight with each other also. One by one,
and two by two, they are all killed. At one
time all are dancing in double combat across
stage and bridge. The Noh fencing with
spear and sword is superb in line. In the
conventional Noh fall, two robbers, facing, who
have killed each other with simultaneous blows,
stand for a moment erect and stiff, then slowly
fall over backward, away from each other, as
stiff as logs, touching the stage at the same
moment with head and heel.

In the play of Atsumori there is an interesting ghost, taken from the epic cycle of the
Yoritomo. Atsumori was a young noble of
the Heike family who was killed in one of

Yoshitsumi's decisive battles. The priest who
opens the final scene tells the story thus :

I am one who serves the great Bishop Homeri
Shonini in Kurodain temple. And that little one
over there is the child of Atsumori, who was killed
at Ichinotani. Once when the Shonini was going
down to the Kamo river, he found a baby about
two years old in a tattered basket under a pine tree.
He felt great pity for the child, took it home with
him, and cared for it tenderly. When the boy had
grown to be ten years of age and was lamenting
that he had no parents, the Shonini spoke about
the matter to an audience which came to his preach-
ing. Then a young woman came up, and cried
excitedly, " This must be my child." On further
enquiry he found it was indeed the child of the
famous Atsumori. The child, having heard all
this, is most desirous to see the image of his father,
even in a dream, and he has been praying devoutly
to this effect at the shrine of Kamo Miojin for
seven days. To-day the term is up for the fulfil-
ment of his vow, so I am taking him down to Kamo
Miojin for his last prayer. Here we are at Kamo.
Now, boy ! pray well !

During his prayer the boy hears a voice
which tells him to go to the forest of Ikuta ;
and thither the priest and the boy journey.
On arrival they look about at the beauty of
the place, till suddenly nightfall surprises them.

" Look here, boy, the sun has set ! What, is that a light yonder ? Perhaps it may be a house ? We will go to take lodging there." A straw hut has been set at the centre of the stage. The curtain in front of it is now withdrawn, and the figure of a very young warrior is disclosed, in a mask, and wearing a dress of blue, white, and gold. He begins to speak to himself :

Gowun ! Gowun ! The five possessions of man are all hollow. Why do we love this queer thing—body ? The soul which dwells in agony flies about like a bat under the moon. The poor bewildered ghost that has lost its body whistles in the autumn wind.

They think him a man, but he tells them he has had a half-hour's respite from hell. He looks wistfully at the boy, who wishes to seize him, and cries, " Flower child of mine, left behind in the world, like a favourite carnation, how pitiful to see you in those old black sleeves ! " Then the spirit dances with restraint, while the chorus chants the martial scene of his former death. " Rushing like two clouds together they were scattered in a whirlwind." Suddenly he stops, looks off the stage, and stamps, shouting :

Who is that over there? A messenger from hell?

Yes, why do you stay so late? King Enma is angry.

Then the grim warriors frantically rush across the stage like Valkyrie, and Atsumori is forced to fight with a spear in a tremendous mystic dance against them. This is a vision of his torment transferred to earth. Exhausted and bleeding he falls; the hell fires vanish; and crying out, " Oh, how shameful that you should see me thus," he melts away from the frantic clutches of the weeping boy.

Among the most weird and delicately poetic pieces is Nishikigi, in which the hero and heroine are the ghosts of two lovers who died unmarried a hundred years before. Their spirits are in the course of the play united near a hillside grave where their bodies had long lain together. This spiritual union is brought about by the piety of a priest. Action, words, and music are vague and ghostly shadows. The lover, as a young man, had waited before the girl's door every night for months, but she, from ignorance or coquetry, had refused to notice him. Then he died of despair. She repented of her cruelty and died also.

FENOLLOSA ON THE NOH

The play opens with the entrance of the
travelling priest, who has wandered to the
ancient village of Kefu in the far north of the
island. He meets the two ghosts in ancient
attire. At first he supposes them to be villagers.
He does not seem to notice their dress, or, if
he does, he apparently mistakes it for some
fashion of the province. Then the two ghosts
sing together, as if muttering to themselves :

We are entangled—whose fault was it, dear ?—
tangled up as the grass patterns are tangled in this
coarse cloth, or that insect which lives and chirrups
in dried seaweed. We do not know where are to-
day our tears in the undergrowth of this eternal
wilderness. We neither wake nor sleep, and
passing our nights in a sorrow, which is in the end
a vision, what are these scenes of spring to us ?
This thinking in sleep of some one who has no
thought for you, is it more than a dream ? And
yet surely it is the natural way of love. In our
hearts there is much and in our bodies nothing, and
we do nothing at all, and only the waters of the
river of tears flow quickly.

Then the priest says :

It is strange, seeing these town-people here. I
might suppose them two married people ; and what
the lady gives herself the trouble of carrying might
be a piece of cloth woven from birds' feathers, and

what the man has is a sword, painted red. It is indeed queer merchandise.

Gradually they tell him the story—they do not say at first that it is their own story. Two people had lived in that village, one of whom had offered the nishikigi, the charm-sticks, the "crimson tokens of love," night after night for three years. That was the man, of course ; and the girl, apparently oblivious, had sat inside her house, weaving long bands of cloth. They say that the man was buried in a cave and all his charm-sticks with him. The priest says it will be a fine tale for him to tell when he gets home, and says he will go see the tomb, to which they offer to guide him. Then the chorus for the first time sings :

The couple are passing in front and the stranger behind, having spent the whole day until dusk, pushing aside the rank grass from the narrow paths about Kefu. Where, indeed, for them is that love-grave ? Ho ! you farmer there, cutting grass upon the hill, tell me clearly how I am to get on further. In this frosty night, of whom shall we ask about the dews on the wayside grass ?

Then the hero, the man's ghost, breaks in for a moment : " Oh how cold it is in these evening dusks of autumn ! " And the chorus resumes :

FENOLLOSA ON THE NOH

Storms, fallen leaves, patches of the autumn showers clogging the feet, the eternal shadow of the long-sloped mountain, and, crying among the ivies on the pine tree, an owl! And as for the love-grave, dyed like the leaves of maple with the tokens of bygone passion, and like the orchids and chrysanthemums which hide the mouth of a fox's hole, they have slipped into the shadow of the cave; this brave couple has vanished into the love-grave.

After an interval, for the changing of the spirits' costumes, the second act begins. The priest cannot sleep in the frost, and thinks he had better pass the night in prayer. Then the spirits in masks steal out, and in mystic language, which he does not hear, try to thank him for his prayer, and say that through his pity the love promise of incarnations long perished is now just realized, even in dream. Then the priest says:

How strange! That place, which seemed like an old grave, is now lighted up from within, and has become like a human dwelling, where people are talking and setting up looms for spinning, and painted sticks. It must be an illusion!

Then follows a wonderful loom song and chorus, comparing the sound of weaving to the clicking of crickets; and in a vision is seen the old tragic story, and the chorus sings that " their tears had become a colour." " But now they shall see the secret bride-room." The hero cries, " And we shall drink the cup of meeting." Then the ghostly chorus sings a final song :

> How glorious the sleeves of the dance
> That are like snow-whirls.

But now the wine-cup of the night-play is reflecting the first hint of the dawn. Perhaps we shall feel awkward when it becomes really morning. And like a dream which is just about to break, the stick and the cloth are breaking up, and the whole place has turned into a deserted grave on a hill, where morning winds are blowing through the pines.

ERNEST FENOLLOSA.
(? about 1906.)

NISHIKIGI [1]

A Play in two Acts, by Motokiyo

CHARACTERS

THE WAKI, a priest.
THE SHITE, or HERO, ghost of the lover.
TSURE, ghost of the woman ; they have both been
    long dead, and have not yet been united.
A CHORUS.

PART FIRST

WAKI

There never was anybody heard of Mt.
Shinobu but had a kindly feeling for it ; so I,
like any other priest that might want to know
a little bit about each one of the provinces,
may as well be walking up here along the
much-travelled road.

I have not yet been about the east country,
but now I have set my mind to go as far as the
earth goes, and why shouldn't I, after all ?

---

[1] The "Nishikigi" are wands used as a love-charm. "Hosonuno" is the name of a local cloth which the woman weaves.

seeing that I go about with my heart set upon no particular place whatsoever, and with no other man's flag in my hand, no more than a cloud has. It is a flag of the night I see coming down upon me. I wonder now, would the sea be that way, or the little place Kefu that they say is stuck down against it.

SHITE AND TSURE

Times out of mind am I here setting up this bright branch, this silky wood with the charms painted in it as fine as the web you'd get in the grass-cloth of Shinobu, that they'd be still selling you in this mountain.

SHITE
(*to* TSURE)

Tangled, we are entangled. Whose fault was it, dear? tangled up as the grass patterns are tangled in this coarse cloth, or as the little Mushi that lives on and chirrups in dried seaweed. We do not know where are to-day our tears in the undergrowth of this eternal wilderness. We neither wake nor sleep, and passing our nights in a sorrow which is in the end a vision, what are these scenes of spring to us? this thinking in sleep of some one who has no thought of you, is it more than a dream? and

132

yet surely it is the natural way of love. In our hearts there is much and in our bodies nothing, and we do nothing at all, and only the waters of the river of tears flow quickly.

Chorus

Narrow is the cloth of Kefu, but wild is that river, that torrent of the hills, between the beloved and the bride.

The cloth she had woven is faded, the thousand one hundred nights were night-trysts watched out in vain.

Waki

(not recognizing the nature of the speakers)

Strange indeed, seeing these town-people here,
They seem like man and wife,
And the lady seems to be holding something
Like a cloth woven of feathers,
While he has a staff or a wooden sceptre
Beautifully ornate.
Both of these things are strange ;
In any case, I wonder what they call them.

Tsure

This is a narrow cloth called "Hosonuno,"
It is just the breadth of the loom.

'NOH'

SHITE

And this is merely wood painted,
And yet the place is famous because of these
    things.
Would you care to buy them from us?

WAKI

Yes, I know that the cloth of this place and
the lacquers are famous things. I have already
heard of their glory, and yet I still wonder why
they have such great reputation.

TSURE

Well now, that's a disappointment. Here
they call the wood " Nishikigi," and the woven
stuff " Hosonuno," and yet you come saying
that you have never heard why, and never
heard the story. Is it reasonable?

SHITE

No, no, that is reasonable enough. What
can people be expected to know of these affairs
when it is more than they can do to keep
abreast of their own?

BOTH
(*to the* PRIEST)

Ah well, you look like a person who has
abandoned the world; it is reasonable enough

that you should not know the worth of wands
and cloths with love's signs painted upon them,
with love's marks painted and dyed.

WAKI

That is a fine answer. And you would tell
me then that Nishikigi and Hosonuno are
names bound over with love?

SHITE

They are names in love's list surely. Every
day for a year, for three years come to their
full, the wands Nishikigi were set up, until
there were a thousand in all. And they are
in song in your time, and will be. " Chid-
zuka " they call them.

TSURE

These names are surely a byword.
As the cloth Hosonuno is narrow of weft,
More narrow than the breast,
We call by this name any woman
Whose breasts are hard to come nigh to.
It is a name in books of love.

SHITE

'Tis a sad name to look back on.

'NOH'

TSURE

A thousand wands were in vain.
A sad name, set in a story.

SHITE

A seed pod void of the seed,
We had no meeting together.

TSURE

Let him read out the story.

CHORUS

At last they forget, they forget.
The wands are no longer offered,
The custom is faded away.
The narrow cloth of Kefu
Will not meet over the breast.
'Tis the story of Hosonuno,
This is the tale :
These bodies, having no weft,
Even now are not come together.
Truly a shameful story,
A tale to bring shame on the gods.

Names of love,
Now for a little spell,
For a faint charm only,
For a charm as slight as the binding together
Of pine-flakes in Iwashiro,

NISHIKIGI

And for saying a wish over them about sunset,
We return, and return to our lodging.
The evening sun leaves a shadow.

WAKI

Go on, tell out all the story.

SHITE

There is an old custom of this country.
We make wands of mediation and deck them
with symbols, and set them before a gate when
we are suitors.

TSURE

And we women take up a wand of the man
we would meet with, and let the others lie,
although a man might come for a hundred
nights, it may be, or for a thousand nights in
three years, till there were a thousand wands
here in the shade of this mountain. We know
the funeral cave of such a man, one who had
watched out the thousand nights ; a bright
cave, for they buried him with all his wands.
They have named it the " Cave of the many
charms."

WAKI

I will go to that love-cave,
It will be a tale to take back to my village.
Will you show me my way there ?

'NOH'

SHITE

So be it, I will teach you the path.

TSURE

Tell him to come over this way.

BOTH

Here are the pair of them
Going along before the traveller.

CHORUS

We have spent the whole day until dusk
Pushing aside the grass
From the overgrown way at Kefu,
And we are not yet come to the cave.
O you there, cutting grass on the hill,
Please set your mind on this matter.
   " You'd be asking where the dew is
   " While the frost's lying here on the road.
   " Who'd tell you that now ? "
Very well, then, don't tell us,
But be sure we will come to the cave.

SHITE

There's a cold feel in the autumn.
Night comes. . . .

CHORUS

And storms ; trees giving up their leaf,
Spotted with sudden showers.

NISHIKIGI

Autumn ! our feet are clogged
In the dew-drenched, entangled leaves.
The perpetual shadow is lonely,
The mountain shadow is lying alone.
The owl cries out from the ivies
That drag their weight on the pine.
Among the orchids and chrysanthemum flowers
The hiding fox is now lord of that love-cave,
Nishidzuka,
That is dyed like the maple's leaf.
They have left us this thing for a saying.
That pair have gone into the cave.
       [*Sign for the exit of* SHITE *and* TSURE.

PART SECOND

(The Waki has taken the posture of sleep.
His respectful visit to the cave is beginning to
have its effect.)

WAKI
(*restless*)

It seems that I cannot sleep
For the length of a pricket's horn.
Under October wind, under pines, under night !
I will do service to Butsu.
       [*He performs the gestures of a ritual.*

'NOH'

Tsure

Aïe, honoured priest !
You do not dip twice in the river
Beneath the same tree's shadow
Without bonds in some other life.
Hear soothsay,
Now is there meeting between us,
Between us who were until now
In life and in after-life kept apart.
A dream-bridge over wild grass,
Over the grass I dwell in.
O honoured ! do not awake me by force.
I see that the law is perfect.

Shite

(*supposedly invisible*)

It is a good service you have done, sir,
A service that spreads in two worlds,
And binds up an ancient love
That was stretched out between them.
I had watched for a thousand days.
I give you largess,
For this meeting is under a difficult law.
And now I will show myself in the form of
    Nishikigi.
I will come out now for the first time in
    colour.

NISHIKIGI

Chorus

The three years are over and past :
All that is but an old story.

Shite

To dream under dream we return.
Three years. . . . And the meeting comes
  now !
This night has happened over and over,
And only now comes the tryst.

Chorus

Look there to the cave
Beneath the stems of the Suzuki.
From under the shadow of the love-grass,
See, see how they come forth and appear
For an instant. . . . Illusion !

Shite

There is at the root of hell
No distinction between princes and commons ;
Wretched for me ! 'tis the saying.

Waki

Strange, what seemed so very old a cave
Is all glittering-bright within,
Like the flicker of fire.
It is like the inside of a house.

141

'NOH'

They are setting up a loom,
And heaping up charm-sticks.   No,
The hangings are out of old time.
Is it illusion, illusion ?

Tsure

Our hearts have been in the dark of the falling
    snow,
We have been astray in the flurry.
You should tell better than we
How much is illusion,
You who are in the world.
We have been in the whirl of those who are
    fading.

Shite

Indeed in old times Narihira said
(And he has vanished with the years),
" Let a man who is in the world tell the fact."
It is for you, traveller,
To say how much is illusion.

Waki

Let it be a dream, or a vision,
Or what you will, I care not.
Only show me the old times over-past and
    snowed under ;
Now, soon, while the night lasts.

NISHIKIGI

SHITE

Look, then, for the old times are shown,
Faint as the shadow-flower shows in the grass
    that bears it ;
And you've but a moon for lanthorn.

TSURE

The woman has gone into the cave.
She sets up her loom there
For the weaving of Hosonuno,
Thin as the heart of Autumn.

SHITE

The suitor for his part, holding his charm-
    sticks,
Knocks on a gate which was barred.

TSURE

In old time he got back no answer,
No secret sound at all
Save . . .

SHITE

    . . . the sound of the loom.

TSURE

It was a sweet sound like katydids and crickets,
A thin sound like the Autumn.

SHITE

It was what you would hear any night.

'NOH'

Kiri.

Shite

Hatari.

Tsure

Cho.

Shite

Cho.

Chorus
(*mimicking the sound of crickets*)

Kiri, hatari, cho, cho,
Kiri, hatari, cho, cho.
The cricket sews on at his old rags,
With all the new grass in the field ; sho,
Churr, isho, like the whirr of a loom : churr.

Chorus
(*antistrophe*)

Let be, they make grass-cloth in Kefu,
Kefu, the land's end, matchless in the world.

Shite

That is an old custom, truly,
But this priest would look on the past.

Chorus

The good priest himself would say :
Even if we weave the cloth, Hosonuno,

NISHIKIGI

And set up the charm-sticks
For a thousand, a hundred nights ;
Even then our beautiful desire will not pass,
Nor fade nor die out.

SHITE

Even to-day the difficulty of our meeting is
    remembered,
And is remembered in song.

CHORUS

That we may acquire power,
Even in our faint substance.
We will show forth even now,
And though it be but in a dream,
Our form of repentance.
> [*Explaining the movement of the* SHITE
> *and* TSURE.

There he is carrying wands,
And she has no need to be asked.
See her within the cave,
With a cricket-like noise of weaving.
The grass-gates and the hedge are between
    them,
That is a symbol.
Night has already come on.
> [*Now explaining the thoughts of the man's
> spirit.*

'NOH'

Love's thoughts are heaped high within him,
As high as the charm-sticks,
As high as the charm-sticks, once coloured,
Now fading, lie heaped in this cave ;
And he knows of their fading. He says :
I lie a body, unknown to any other man,
Like old wood buried in moss.
It were a fit thing
That I should stop thinking the love-thoughts,
The charm-sticks fade and decay,
And yet,
The rumour of our love
Takes foot, and moves through the world.
We had no meeting.
But tears have, it seems, brought out a bright
  blossom
Upon the dyed tree of love.

Shite

Tell me, could I have foreseen
Or known what a heap of my writings
Should lie at the end of her shaft-bench ?

Chorus

A hundred nights and more
Of twisting, encumbered sleep,
And now they make it a ballad,

NISHIKIGI

Not for one year or for two only,
But until the days lie deep
As the sand's depth at Kefu.
Until the year's end is red with autumn,
Red like these love-wands,
A thousand nights are in vain.
I, too, stand at this gate-side :
You grant no admission, you do not show
    yourself
Until I and my sleeves are faded.
By the dew-like gemming of tears upon my
    sleeve,
Why will you grant no admission ?
And we all are doomed to pass
You, and my sleeves and my tears.
And you did not even know when three years
    had come to an end.
Cruel, ah, cruel !
The charm-sticks . . .

Shite

    . . . were set up a thousand times ;
Then, now, and for always.

Chorus

Shall I ever at last see into that secret bride-
    room, which no other sight has traversed ?

'NOH'

SHITE

Happy at last and well-starred,
Now comes the eve of betrothal :
We meet for the wine-cup.

CHORUS

How glorious the sleeves of the dance,
That are like snow-whirls !

SHITE

Tread out the dance.

CHORUS

Tread out the dance and bring music.
This dance is for Nishikigi.

SHITE

This dance is for the evening plays,
And for the weaving.

CHORUS

For the tokens between lover and lover :
It is a reflecting in the wine-cup.

CHORUS

Ari-aki,
The dawn !
Come, we are out of place ;
Let us go ere the light comes.

[To the WAKI.

NISHIKIGI

We ask you, do not awake,
We all will wither away,
The wands and this cloth of a dream.
Now you will come out of sleep,
You tread the border and nothing
Awaits you : no, all this will wither away.
There is nothing here but this cave in the
     field's midst.
To-day's wind moves in the pines ;
A wild place, unlit, and unfilled.

FINIS

KINUTA

CHARACTERS

WAKI, a country gentleman.
TSURE, the servant-maid YUGIRI.
SHITE, the wife.
SECOND SHITE, ghost of the wife.

In Kinuta (" The Silk-board ") the plot is
as follows :

The Waki, a country gentleman, has tarried
long in the capital. He at last sends the Tsure,
a maid-servant, home with a message to his
wife. The servant talks on the road. She
reaches the Waki's house and talks with the
Shite (the wife). The chorus comments.
Finally, the wife dies. The chorus sing a
death-song, after which the husband returns.
The second Shite, the ghost of the wife, then
appears, and continues speaking alternately
with the chorus until the close.

HUSBAND

I am of Ashiya of Kinshu, unknown and of
no repute. I have been loitering on in the

capital entangled in many litigations. I went
for a casual visit, and there I have been tarrying
for three full years. Now I am anxious, over-
anxious, about affairs in my home. I shall
send Yugiri homeward ; she is a maid in my
employ. Ho ! Yugiri ! I am worried. I
shall send you down to the country. You
will go home and tell them that I return at
the end of this year.

MAID-SERVANT

I will go, Sir, and say that then you are
surely coming. (*She starts on her journey.*)
The day is advancing, and I, in my travelling
clothes, travel with the day. I do not know
the lodgings, I do not know the dreams upon
the road, I do not know the number of the
dreams that gather for one night's pillow. At
length I am come to the village—it is true
that I was in haste—I am come at last to
Ashiya. I think I will call out gently. " Is
there any person or thing in this house ? Say
that Yugiri is here in the street, she has just
come back from the city."

WIFE

Sorrow !—
Sorrow is in the twigs of the duck's nest
And in the pillow of the fishes,

KINUTA

At being held apart in the waves,
Sorrow between mandarin ducks,
Who have been in love
Since time out of mind.
Sorrow—
There is more sorrow between the united
Though they move in the one same world.
O low " Remembering-grass,"
I do not forget to weep
At the sound of the rain upon you,
My tears are a rain in the silence,
O heart of the seldom clearing.

MAID-SERVANT

Say to whomsoever it concerns that Yugiri
has come.

WIFE

What ! you say it is Yugiri ? There is no
need for a servant. Come to this side ! in
here ! How is this, Yugiri, that you are so
great a stranger ? Yet welcome. I have cause
of complaint. If you were utterly changed,
why did you send me no word ? Not even a
message in the current of the wind ?

MAID-SERVANT

Truly I wished to come, but his Honour

gave me no leisure. For three years he kept
me in that very ancient city.

Wife

You say it was against your heart to stay
in the city ? While even in the time of delights
I thought of its blossom, until sorrow had
grown the cloak of my heart.

Chorus

As the decline of autumn
In a country dwelling,
With the grasses failing and fading—
As men's eyes fail—
As men's eyes fail,
Love has utterly ceased.
Upon what shall she lean to-morrow ?
A dream of the autumn, three years,
Until the sorrow of those dreams awakes
Autumnal echoes within her.
Now former days are changed,
They have left no shadow or trace ;
And if there were no lies in all the world
Then there might come some pleasure
Upon the track of men's words.
Alas, for her foolish heart !
How foolish her trust has been.

KINUTA

Wife

What strange thing is it beyond there that takes the forms of sound ? Tell me. What is it ?

Maid-servant

A villager beating a silk-board.

Wife

Is that all ? And I am weary as an old saying. When the wandering Sobu [1] of China was in the Mongol country he also had left a wife and children, and she, aroused upon the clear cold nights, climbed her high tower and beat such a silk-board, and had perhaps some purpose of her heart. For that far-murmuring cloth could move his sleep—that is the tale — though he were leagues away. Yet I have stretched my board with patterned cloths, which curious birds brought through the twilit utter solitude, and hoped with such that I might ease my heart.

Maid-servant

Boards are rough work, hard even for the poor, and you of high rank have done this to ease your heart ! Here, let me arrange them, I am better fit for such business.

[1] So Wu.

'NOH'

Wife

Beat then. Beat out our resentment.

Maid-servant

It's a coarse mat ; we can never be sure.

Chorus

The voice of the pine-trees sinks ever into the
    web !
The voice of the pine-trees, now falling,
Shall make talk in the night.
It is cold.

Wife

Autumn it is, and news rarely comes in
your fickle wind, the frost comes bearing no
message.

Chorus

Weariness tells of the night.

Wife

Even a man in a very far village might
see. . . .

Chorus

Perhaps the moon will not call upon her,
saying : " Whose night-world is this ? "

KINUTA

WIFE

O beautiful season, say also this time is
toward autumn, " The evening moves to an
end."

CHORUS

The stag's voice has bent her heart toward
    sorrow,
Sending the evening winds which she does
    not see,
We cannot see the tip of the branch.
The last leaf falls without witness.
There is an awe in the shadow,
And even the moon is quiet,
With the love-grass under the eaves.

WIFE

My blind soul hangs like a curtain studded
with dew.

CHORUS

What a night to unsheave her sorrows—
An hour for magic—
And that cloth-frame stands high on the palace ;
The wind rakes it from the north.

WIFE

They beat now fast and now slow—are
they silk-workers down in the village ? The
moon-river pours on the west.

'NOH'

Chorus
(strophe)

The wandering Sobu is asleep in the North
    country,
And here in the East-sky the autumnal wind is
    working about from the West.
Wind, take up the sound she is beating upon
    her coarse-webbed cloth.

Chorus
(antistrophe)

Beware of even the pines about the eaves,
Lest they confuse the sound.
Beware that you do not lose the sound of the
    travelling storm,
That travels after your travels.
Take up the sound of this beating of the cloths.
    Go where her lord is, O Wind ; my heart
reaches out and can be seen by him ; I pray
that you keep him still dreaming.

Wife

    Aoi ! if the web is broken, who, weary
with time, will then come to seek me out ?
If at last he should come to seek me, let him
call in the deep of time. Cloths are changed
by recutting, hateful ! love thin as a summer
cloth ! Let my lord's life be even so slight,

KINUTA

for I have no sleep under the moon. O let
me go on with my cloths !

Chorus

The love of a god with a goddess
Is but for the one night in passing,
So thin are the summer cloths !
The river-waves of the sky
Have cut through our time like shears,
They have kept us apart with dew.
There are tears on the Kaji leaf,
There is dew upon the helm-bar
Of the skiff in the twisting current.
Will it harm the two sleeves of the gods
If he pass ?
As a floating shadow of the water grass,
That the ripples break on the shore ?
O foam, let him be as brief.

Wife

The seventh month is come to its seventh
day ; we are hard on the time of long nights,
and I would send him the sadness of these ten
thousand voices—the colour of the moon, the
breath-colour of the wind, even the points of
frost that assemble in the shadow. A time
that brings awe to the heart, a sound of beaten
cloths, and storms in the night, a crying in

the storm, a sad sound of the crickets, make one sound in the falling dew, a whispering lamentation, hera, hera, a sound in the cloth of beauty.

MAID-SERVANT

What shall I say to all this? A man has just come from the city. The master will not come this year. It seems as if . . .

CHORUS

The heart, that thinks that it will think no more, grows fainter; outside in the withered field the crickets' noise has gone faint. The flower lies open to the wind, the gazers pass on to madness, this flower-heart of the grass is blown on by a wind-like madness, until at last she is but emptiness.

[*The wife dies. Enter the husband, returning.*

HUSBAND

Pitiful hate, for my three years' delay, working within her has turned our long-drawn play of separation to separation indeed.

CHORUS

The time of regret comes not before the deed, This we have heard from the eight thousand shadows.

KINUTA

This is their chorus—the shadowy blades of
    grass.
Sorrow ! to be exchanging words
At the string-tip—
Sorrow ! that we can but speak
With the bow-tip of the adzusa !
The way that a ghost returns
From the shadow of the grass—
We have heard the stories,
It is eight thousand times, they say,
Before regret runs in a smooth-worn groove,
Forestalls itself.

Ghost of the Wife

Aoi ! for fate, fading, alas, and unformed,
all sunk into the river of three currents, gone
from the light of the plum flowers that reveal
spring in the world !

Chorus

She has but kindling flame to light her
track . . .

Ghost of the Wife

. . . and show her autumns of a lasting moon.[1]
And yet, who had not fallen into desire ? It
was easy, in the rising and falling of the smoke

---

[1] I.e. a moon that has no phases.

and the fire of thought, to sink so deep in desires. O heart, you were entangled in the threads. " Suffering " and " the Price " are their names. There is no end to the lashes of Aborasetsu, the jailor of this prison. O heart, in your utter extremity you beat the silks of remorse ; to the end of all false desire Karma shows her hate.

Chorus

Ah false desire and fate !
Her tears are shed on the silk-board,
Tears fall and turn into flame,
The smoke has stifled her cries,
She cannot reach us at all,
Nor yet the beating of the silk-board
Nor even the voice of the pines,
But only the voice of that sorrowful punishment.
Aoi ! Aoi !

Slow as the pace of sleep,
Swift as the steeds of time,
By the six roads of changing and passing
We do not escape from the wheel,
Nor from the flaming of Karma,
Though we wander through life and death ;
This woman fled from his horses
To a world without taste or breath.

KINUTA

Ghost of the Wife

Even the leaves of the katsu-grass show their hate of this underworld by the turning away of their leaves.

Chorus

The leaves of the katsu show their hate by bending aside ; and neither can they unbend nor can the face of o'ershadowed desire. O face of eagerness, though you had loved him truly through both worlds, and hope had clung a thousand generations, 'twere little avail. The cliffs of Matsuyama, with stiff pines, stand in the end of time ; your useless speech is but false mocking, like the elfish waves. Aoi ! Aoi ! Is this the heart of man ?

Ghost of the Wife

It is the great, false bird called "Taking-care."

Chorus

Who will call him a true man—the wandering husband—when even the plants know their season, the feathered and furred have their hearts ? It seems that our story has set a fact beyond fable. Even Sobu, afar, gave to the flying wild-duck a message to be borne through the southern country, over a thousand leagues, so deep was his heart's current—not shallow the love in his heart. Kimi, you have no drowsy thought of me, and no dream of yours reaches toward me. Hateful, and why ? O hateful !

Chorus

She recites the Flower of Law ; the ghost is received into Butsu ; the road has become enlightened. Her constant beating of silk has opened the flower, even so lightly she has entered the seed-pod of Butsu.

FINIS

HAGOROMO

A Play in one Act

<small>CHARACTERS</small>

CHIEF FISHERMAN, HAKURYO.
A FISHERMAN.
A TENNIN.
CHORUS.

The plot of the play Hagoromo, the Feather-mantle, is as follows: The priest finds the Hagoromo, the magical feather-mantle of a Tennin, an aerial spirit or celestial dancer, hanging upon a bough. She demands its return. He argues with her, and finally promises to return it, if she will teach him her dance or part of it. She accepts the offer. The Chorus explains the dance as symbolical of the daily changes of the moon. The words about " three, five, and fifteen " refer to the number of nights in the moon's changes. In the finale, the Tennin is supposed to disappear like a mountain slowly hidden in mist. The play shows the relation of the early Noh to the God-dance.

HAKURYO

Windy road of the waves by Miwo,
Swift with ships, loud over steersmen's voices.

Hakuryo, taker of fish, head of his house, dwells upon the barren pine-waste of Miwo.

A FISHERMAN

Upon a thousand heights had gathered the inexplicable cloud. Swept by the rain, the moon is just come to light the high house.

A clean and pleasant time surely. There comes the breath-colour of spring ; the waves rise in a line below the early mist ; the moon is still delaying above, though we've no skill to grasp it. Here is a beauty to set the mind above itself.

CHORUS

I shall not be out of memory
Of the mountain road by Kiyomi,
Nor of the parted grass by that bay,
Nor of the far seen pine-waste
Of Miwo of wheat stalks.

Let us go according to custom. Take hands against the wind here, for it presses the clouds and the sea. Those men who were going to fish are about to return without

launching. Wait a little, is it not spring?
will not the wind be quiet? This wind is only
the voice of the lasting pine-trees, ready for
stillness. See how the air is soundless, or
would be, were it not for the waves. There
now, the fishermen are putting out with even
the smallest boats.

HAKURYO

I am come to shore at Miwo-no; I dis-
embark in Matsubara; I see all that they
speak of on the shore. An empty sky with
music, a rain of flowers, strange fragrance on
every side; all these are no common things,
nor is this cloak that hangs upon the pine-
tree. As I approach to inhale its colour, I am
aware of mystery. Its colour-smell is mysterious. I see that it is surely no common dress.
I will take it now and return and make it a
treasure in my house, to show to the aged.

TENNIN

That cloak belongs to some one on this
side. What are you proposing to do with it?

HAKURYO

This? this is a cloak picked up. I am
taking it home, I tell you.

'NOH'

TENNIN

That is a feather-mantle not fit for a mortal
    to bear,
Not easily wrested from the sky-traversing
    spirit,
Not easily taken or given.
I ask you to leave it where you found it.

HAKURYO

How! Is the owner of this cloak a Tennin?
So be it. In this downcast age I should keep
it, a rare thing, and make it a treasure in the
country, a thing respected. Then I should
not return it.

TENNIN

Pitiful, there is no flying without the cloak
of feathers, no return through the ether. I
pray you return me the mantle.

HAKURYO

Just from hearing these high words, I,
Hakuryo, have gathered more and yet more
force. You think, because I was too stupid
to recognize it, that I shall be unable to take
and keep hid the feather-robe, that I shall
give it back for merely being told to stand and
withdraw?

HAGOROMO

Tennin

A Tennin without her robe,
A bird without wings,
How shall she climb the air ?

Hakuryo

And this world would be a sorry place for
her to dwell in ?

Tennin

I am caught, I struggle, how shall I . . . ?

Hakuryo

No, Hakuryo is not one to give back the
robe.

Tennin

Power does not attain . . .

Hakuryo

. . . to get back the robe. . . .

Chorus

Her coronet,[1] jewelled as with the dew of
tears, even the flowers that decorated her hair,
drooping and fading, the whole chain of
weaknesses [2] of the dying Tennin can be seen
actually before the eyes.   Sorrow !

---

[1] Vide examples of state head-dress of kingfisher feathers in
the South Kensington Museum.

[2] The chain of weaknesses, or the five ills, diseases of the

'NOH'

TENNIN

I look into the flat of heaven, peering ;
the cloud-road is all hidden and uncertain ; we
are lost in the rising mist ; I have lost the
knowledge of the road. Strange, a strange
sorrow !

CHORUS

Enviable colour of breath, wonder of clouds
that fade along the sky that was our accustomed
dwelling ; hearing the sky-bird, accustomed,
and well accustomed, hearing the voices grow
fewer, the wild geese fewer and fewer, along
the highways of air, how deep her longing
to return ! Plover and seagull are on the waves
in the offing. Do they go or do they return ?
She reaches out for the very blowing of the
spring wind against heaven.

HAKURYO
(*to the* TENNIN)

What do you say ? Now that I can see
you in your sorrow, gracious, of heaven, I
bend and would return you your mantle.

TENNIN

It grows clearer. No, give it this side.

Tennin : namely, the Tamakadzura withers ; the Hagoromo is
stained ; sweat comes from the body ; both eyes wink frequently ;
she feels very weary of her palace in heaven.

HAGOROMO

Hakuryo

First tell me your nature, who are you, Tennin ? Give payment with the dance of the Tennin, and I will return you your mantle.

Tennin

Readily and gladly, and then I return into heaven. You shall have what pleasure you will, and I will leave a dance here, a joy to be new among men and to be memorial dancing. Learn then this dance that can turn the palace of the moon. No, come here to learn it. For the sorrows of the world I will leave this new dancing with you for sorrowful people. But give me my mantle, I cannot do the dance rightly without it.

Hakuryo

Not yet, for if you should get it, how do I know you'll not be off to your palace without even beginning your dance, not even a measure?

Tennin

Doubt is fitting for mortals ; with us there is no deceit.

Hakuryo

I am again ashamed. I give you your mantle.

'NOH'

CHORUS

The young sprite now is arrayed, she assumes the curious mantle ; watch how she moves in the dance of the rainbow-feathered garment.

HAKURYO

The heavenly feather-robe moves in accord with the wind.

TENNIN

The sleeves of flowers are being wet with the rain.

HAKURYO

All three are doing one step.

CHORUS

It seems that she dances.
Thus was the dance of pleasure,
Suruga dancing, brought to the sacred east.
Thus was it when the lords of the everlasting
Trod the world,
They being of old our friends.
Upon ten sides their sky is without limit,
They have named it, on this account, the
enduring.

TENNIN

The jewelled axe takes up the eternal renewing, the palace of the moon-god is being renewed with the jewelled axe, and this is always recurring.

172

HAGOROMO

Chorus

(commenting on the dance)

The white kiromo, the black kiromo,
Three, five into fifteen,
The figure that the Tennin is dividing.
There are heavenly nymphs, Amaotome,[1]
One for each night of the month,
And each with her deed assigned.

Tennin

I also am heaven-born and a maid, Amaotome. Of them there are many. This is the
dividing of my body, that is fruit of the moon's
tree, Katsura.[2] This is one part of our dance
that I leave to you here in your world.

Chorus

The spring mist is widespread abroad ; so
perhaps the wild olive's flower will blossom
in the infinitely unreachable moon. Her
flowery head-ornament is putting on colour ;
this truly is sign of the spring. Not sky is
here, but the beauty ; and even here comes
the heavenly, wonderful wind. O blow, shut
the accustomed path of the clouds. O, you

---

[1] Cf. "Paradiso," xxiii. 25 :
> "Quale nei plenilunii sereni
> Trivia ride tra le ninfe eterne."

[2] A tree something like the laurel.

in the form of a maid, grant us the favour of
your delaying. The pine-waste of Miwo puts
on the colour of spring. The bay of Kiyomi
lies clear before the snow upon Fuji. Are
not all these presages of the spring? There
are but few ripples beneath the piny wind. It
is quiet along the shore. There is naught
but a fence of jewels between the earth and
the sky, and the gods within and without,[1]
beyond and beneath the stars, and the moon
unclouded by her lord, and we who are born
of the sun. This alone intervenes, here where
the moon is unshadowed, here in Nippon, the
sun's field.

TENNIN

The plumage of heaven drops neither
feather nor flame to its own diminution.

CHORUS

Nor is this rock of earth overmuch worn
by the brushing of that feather-mantle, the
feathery skirt of the stars : rarely, how rarely.
There is a magic song from the east, the voices
of many and many : and flute and sho, filling
the space beyond the cloud's edge, seven-
stringed ; dance filling and filling. The red
sun blots on the sky the line of the colour-

---

[1] "Within and without," gei, gu, two parts of the temple.

drenched mountains. The flowers rain in a gust ; it is no racking storm that comes over this green moor, which is afloat, as it would seem, in these waves.

Wonderful is the sleeve of the white cloud, whirling such snow here.

Tennin

Plain of life, field of the sun, true foundation, great power !

Chorus

Hence and for ever this dancing shall be called " a revel in the East." Many are the robes thou hast, now of the sky's colour itself, and now a green garment.

Semi-Chorus

And now the robe of mist, presaging spring, a colour-smell as this wonderful maiden's skirt— left, right, left ! The rustling of flowers, the putting on of the feathery sleeve ; they bend in air with the dancing.

Semi-Chorus

Many are the joys in the east. She who is the colour-person of the moon takes her middle-night in the sky. She marks her three fives with this dancing, as a shadow of all fulfil-

175

ments. The circled vows are at full. Give the
seven jewels of rain and all of the treasure, you
who go from us. After a little time, only a
little time, can the mantle be upon the wind
that was spread over Matsubara or over Ashitaka
the mountain, though the clouds lie in its
heaven like a plain awash with sea. Fuji is
gone ; the great peak of Fuji is blotted out
little by little. It melts into the upper mist.
In this way she (the Tennin) is lost to sight.

FINIS

KAGEKIYO

A Play in one Act, by Motokiyo

CHARACTERS

SHITE, KAGEKIYO old and blind.
TSURE, a girl, his daughter, called HITOMARU.
TOMO, her attendant.
WAKI, a villager.
The scene is in HIUGA.

GIRL AND ATTENDANT
(*chanting*)

What should it be ; the body of dew, wholly
at the mercy of wind ?

GIRL

I am a girl named Hitomaru from the river
    valley Kamegaye-ga-Yatsu,
My father, Akushichi-bioye Kagekiyo,
Fought by the side of Heike,
And is therefore hated by Genji.
He was banished to Miyazaki in Hiuga,
To waste out the end of his life.

'NOH'

Though I am unaccustomed to travel,
I will try to go to my father.

GIRL AND ATTENDANT
*(describing the journey as they walk
across the bridge and the stage)*

Sleeping with the grass for our pillow,
The dew has covered our sleeves.

[Singing.

Of whom shall I ask my way
As I go out from Sagami province ?
Of whom in Totomi ?
I crossed the bay in a small hired boat
And came to Yatsuhashi in Mikawa ;
Ah, when shall I see the City-on-the-cloud ?

ATTENDANT

As we have come so fast, we are now in
Miyazaki of Hiuga.
It is here you should ask for your father.

KAGEKIYO
(in another corner of the stage)

Sitting at the gate of the pine wood I wear
out the end of my years. I cannot see the clear
light, I do not know how the time passes. I
sit here in this dark hovel, with one coat for

KAGEKIYO

the warm and the cold, and my body is but a framework of bones.

CHORUS

May as well be a priest with black sleeves. Now having left the world in sorrow, I look upon my withered shape. There is no one to pity me now.

GIRL

Surely no one can live in that ruin, and yet a voice sounds from it. A beggar, perhaps. Let us take a few steps and see.

KAGEKIYO

My eyes will not show it me, yet the autumn wind is upon us.

GIRL

The wind blows from an unknown past, and spreads our doubts through the world. The wind blows, and I have no rest, nor any place to find quiet.

KAGEKIYO

Neither in the world of passion, nor in the world of colour, nor in the world of non-colour, is there any such place of rest; beneath the one sky are they all. Whom shall I ask, and how answer?

GIRL

Shall I ask the old man by the thatch ?

KAGEKIYO

Who are you ?

GIRL

Where does the exile live ?

KAGEKIYO

What exile ?

GIRL

One who is called Akushichi-bioye Kage-kiyo, a noble who fought with Heike.

KAGEKIYO

Indeed ? I have heard of him, but I am blind, I have not looked in his face. I have heard of his wretched condition and pity him. You had better ask for him at the next place.

ATTENDANT

(*to girl*)

It seems that he is not here, shall we ask further ?   [*They pass on.*

KAGEKIYO

Strange, I feel that woman who has just passed is the child of that blind man. Long

ago I loved a courtesan in Atsuta, one time
when I was in that place. But I thought our
girl-child would be no use to us, and I left
her with the head man in the valley of Kame-
gaye-ga-yatsu ; and now she has gone by me
and spoken, although she does not know who
I am.

CHORUS

Although I have heard her voice,
The pity is, that I cannot see her.
And I have let her go by
Without divulging my name.
This is the true love of a father.

ATTENDANT
(*at further side of the stage*)
Is there any native about ?

VILLAGER
What do you want with me ?

ATTENDANT
Do you know where the exile lives ?

VILLAGER
What exile is it you want ?

ATTENDANT
Akushichi-bioye Kagekiyo, a noble of
Heike's party.

'NOH'

Villager

Did not you pass an old man under the edge of the mountain as you were coming that way?

Attendant

A blind beggar in a thatched cottage.

Villager

That fellow was Kagekiyo. What ails the lady, she shivers?

Attendant

A question you might well ask, she is the exile's daughter. She wanted to see her father once more, and so came hither to seek him. Will you take us to Kagekiyo?

Villager

Bless my soul! Kagekiyo's daughter. Come, come, never mind, young miss. Now I will tell you, Kagekiyo went blind in both eyes, and so he shaved his crown and called himself " The blind man of Hiuga." He begs a bit from the passers, and the likes of us keep him; he'd be ashamed to tell you his name. However, I'll come along with you, and then I'll call out, " Kagekiyo!" and if he comes, you can see him and have a word with him. Let us along. (*They cross the stage, and the villager calls*) Kagekiyo! Oh, there, Kage-kiyo!

KAGEKIYO

Noise, noise! Some one came from my home to call me, but I sent them on. I couldn't be seen like this. Tears like the thousand lines in a rain storm, bitter tears soften my sleeve. Ten thousand things rise in a dream, and I wake in this hovel, wretched, just a nothing in the wide world. How can I answer when they call me by my right name?

CHORUS

Do not call out the name he had in his glory. You will move the bad blood in his heart. (*Then, taking up* KAGEKIYO's *thought*) I am angry.

KAGEKIYO

Living here . . .

CHORUS

(*going on with* KAGEKIYO's *thought*)

I go on living here, hated by the people in power. A blind man without his staff. I am deformed, and therefore speak evil; excuse me.

KAGEKIYO

My eyes are darkened.

183

' NOH '

Chorus

Though my eyes are dark I understand the thoughts of another. I understand at a word. The wind comes down from the pine trees on the mountain, and snow comes down after the wind. The dream tells of my glory. I am loath to wake from the dream. I hear the waves running in the evening tide, as when I was with Heike. Shall I act out the old ballad ?

Kagekiyo
(*to the villager*)

I had a weight on my mind, I spoke to you very harshly ; excuse me.

Villager

You're always like that, never mind it. Has any one been here to see you ?

Kagekiyo

No one but you.

Villager

Go on ! That is not true. Your daughter was here. Why couldn't you tell her the truth, she being so sad and so eager ? I have brought her back now. Come now, speak with your father. Come along.

KAGEKIYO

GIRL

Oh, Oh, I came such a long journey, under rain, under wind, wet with dew, over the frost; you do not see into my heart. It seems that a father's love goes when the child is not worth it.

KAGEKIYO

I meant to keep it concealed, but now they have found it all out. I shall drench you with the dew of my shame, you who are young as a flower. I tell you my name, and that we are father and child, yet I thought this would put dishonour upon you, and therefore I let you pass. Do not hold it against me.

CHORUS

At first I was angry that my friends would no longer come near me. But now I have come to a time when I could not believe that even a child of my own would seek me out.

[*Singing*.

Upon all the boats of the men of Heike's
    faction
Kagekiyo was the fighter most in call,
Brave were his men, cunning sailors,
And now even the leader
Is worn out and dull as a horse.

'NOH'

VILLAGER
(*to* KAGEKIYO)

Many a fine thing is gone, sir, your daughter
would like to ask you. . . .

KAGEKIYO

What is it?

VILLAGER

She has heard of your fame from the old
days. Would you tell her the ballad?

KAGEKIYO

Towards the end of the third month, it was
in the third year of Juei. We men of Heike
were in ships, the men of Genji were on land.
Their war-tents stretched on the shore. We
awaited decision. And Noto-no-Kami Noritsune said : " Last year in the hills of Harima,
and in Midzushima, and in Hiyodorigoye of
Bitchiu, we were defeated time and again, for
Yoshitsune is tactful and cunning. Is there
any way we can beat them? " Kagekiyo
thought in his mind : " This Hangan Yoshitsune is neither god nor a devil, at the risk of
my life I might do it." So he took leave of
Noritsune and led a party against the shore,
and all the men of Genji rushed on them.

KAGEKIYO

Chorus

Kagekiyo cried, "You are haughty." His armour caught every turn of the sun. He drove them four ways before them.

Kagekiyo
(*excited and crying out*)

Samoshiya ! Run, cowards !

Chorus

He thought, how easy this killing. He rushed with his spear-haft gripped under his arm. He cried out, "I am Kagekiyo of the Heike." He rushed on to take them. He pierced through the helmet vizards of Miyonoya. Miyonoya fled twice, and again ; and Kagekiyo cried : " You shall not escape me ! " He leaped and wrenched off his helmet. " Eya ! " The vizard broke and remained in his hand and Miyonoya still fled afar, and afar, and he looked back crying in terror, " How terrible, how heavy your arm ! " And Kagekiyo called at him, " How tough the shaft of your neck is ! " And they both laughed out over the battle, and went off each his own way.

Chorus

These were the deeds of old, but oh, to tell them ! to be telling them over now in his wretched condition. His life in the world is weary, he is near the end of his course. "Go back," he would say to his daughter. "Pray for me when I am gone from the world, for I shall then count upon you as we count on a lamp in the darkness . . . we who are blind." "I will stay," she said. Then she obeyed him, and only one voice is left.

We tell this for the remembrance. Thus were the parent and child.

FINIS

NOTE

Fenollosa has left this memorandum on the stoicism of the last play : I asked Mr. Hirata how it could be considered natural or dutiful for the daughter to leave her father in such a condition. He said, " that the Japanese would not be in sympathy with such sternness now, but that it was the old Bushido spirit. The personality of the old man is worn out, no more good in this life. It would be sentimentality for her to remain with him. No good could be done. He could well restrain his love for her, better that she should pray for him and go on with the work of her normal life."

PART IV

PART IV

I GIVE the next two plays, Awoi no Uye and Kakitsubata, with very considerable diffidence. I am not sure that they are clear ; Japanese with whom I have discussed them do not seem able to give me much help. Several passages which are, however, quite lucid in themselves, seem to me as beautiful as anything I have found in Fenollosa's Japanese notes, and these passages must be my justification. In each case I give an explanation of the story so far as I understand it. In one place in Kakitsubata I have transferred a refrain or doubled it. For the rest the plays are as literal as the notes before me permit.

AWOI NO UYE
A Play by Ujinobu

INTRODUCTION

THE story, as I understand it, is that the
" Court Lady Awoi " (Flower of the East) is
jealous of the other and later co-wives of
Genji. This jealousy reaches its climax, and
she goes off her head with it, when her carriage
is overturned and broken at the Kami festival.
The play opens with the death-bed of Awoi,
and in Mrs. Fenollosa's diary I find the statement that " Awoi, her struggles, sickness, and
death are represented by a red, flowered
kimono, folded once length-wise, and laid at
the front edge of the stage."

The objective action is confined to the
apparitions and exorcists. The demon of
jealousy, tormenting Awoi, first appears in
the form of the Princess Rakujo, then with the
progress and success of the exorcism the jealous

quintessence is driven out of this personal
ghost, and appears in its own truly demonic
(" hannya ") form—" That awful face with
its golden eyes and horns revealed." The
exorcist Miko is powerless against this demon,
but the yamabushi exorcists, " advancing
against it, making a grinding noise with the
beads of their rosaries and striking against it,"
finally drive it away.

The ambiguities of certain early parts of
the play seem mainly due to the fact that the
" Princess Rokujo," the concrete figure on the
stage, is a phantom or image of Awoi no
Uye's own jealousy. That is to say, Awoi is
tormented by her own passion, and this passion
obsesses her first in the form of a personal
apparition of Rokujo, then in demonic form.

This play was written before Ibsen declared
that life is a " contest with the phantoms of
the mind." The difficulties of the translator
have lain in separating what belongs to Awoi
herself from the things belonging to the ghost
of Rokujo, very much as modern psychologists
might have difficulty in detaching the personality or memories of an obsessed person
from the personal memories of the obsession.
Baldly : an obsessed person thinks he is
Napoleon ; an image of his own thought

would be confused with scraps relating perhaps to St. Helena, Corsica, and Waterloo.

The second confusion is the relation of the two apparitions. It seems difficult to make it clear that the " hannya " has been cast out of the ghostly personality, and that it had been, in a way, the motive force in the ghost's actions. And again we cannot make it too clear that the ghost is not actually a separate soul, but only a manifestation made possible through Awoi and her passion of jealousy. At least with this interpretation the play seems moderately coherent and lucid.

Rokujo or Awoi, whichever we choose to consider her, comes out of hell-gate in a chariot, " because people of her rank are always accustomed to go about in chariots. When they, or their ghosts, think of motion, they think of going in a chariot, therefore they take that form." There would be a model chariot shown somewhere at the back of the stage.

The ambiguity of the apparition's opening line is, possibly, to arouse the curiosity of the audience. There will be an air of mystery, and they will not know whether it is to be the chariot associated with Genji's liaison with Yugawo, the beautiful heroine of the play

Hajitomi, or whether it is the symbolic chariot
drawn by a sheep, a deer, and an ox. But I
think we are nearer the mark if we take Rokujo's
enigmatic line, " I am come in three chariots,"
to mean that the formed idea of a chariot is
derived from these events and from the mishap
to Awoi's own chariot, all of which have combined and helped the spirit world to manifest
itself concretely. Western students of ghostly
folk-lore would tell you that the world of spirits
is fluid and drifts about seeking shape. I do
not wish to dogmatize on these points.

The Fenollosa-Hirata draft calls the manifest
spirit " The Princess Rokujo," and she attacks
Awoi, who is represented by the folded kimono.
Other texts seem to call this manifestation
" Awoi no Uye," i.e. her mind or troubled
spirit, and this spirit attacks her body. It will
be perhaps simpler for the reader if I mark her
speeches simply " Apparition," and those of
the second form " Hannya."

I do not know whether I can make the
matter more plain or summarize it otherwise
than by saying that the whole play is a drama-
tization, or externalization, of Awoi's jealousy.
The passion makes her subject to the demon-
possession. The demon first comes in a disguised and beautiful form. The prayer of

the exorcist forces him first to appear in his true shape, and then to retreat.

But the " disguised and beautiful form " is not a mere abstract sheet of matter. It is a sort of personal or living mask, having a ghost-life of its own ; it is at once a shell of the princess, and a form, which is strengthened or made more palpable by the passion of Awoi.

AWOI NO UYE

Scene in Kioto

DAIJIN

I am a subject in the service of the Blessed Emperor Shujakuin. They have called in the priests and the high priests for the sickness of Awoi no Uye of the house of Sadaijin. They prayed, but the gods give no sign. I am sent to Miko, the wise, to bid him pray to the spirits. Miko, will you pray to the earth ?

MIKO

Tenshojo, chishojo,
Naigeshojo, Rakkonshojo.

Earth, pure earth,
Wither, by the sixteen roots
(Wither this evil) !

197

'NOH'

APPARITION

It may be, it may be, I come from the gate of hell in three coaches. I am sorry for Yugawo and the carriage with broken wheels. And the world is ploughed with sorrow as a field is furrowed with oxen. Man's life is a wheel on the axle, there is no turn whereby to escape. His hold is light as dew on the Basho leaf. It seems that the last spring's blossoms are only a dream in the mind. And we fools take it all, take it all as a matter of course. Oh, I am grown envious from sorrow. I come to seek consolation. (*Singing.*) Though I lie all night hid for shame in the secret carriage, looking at the moon for sorrow, yet I would not be seen by the moon.

> Where Miko draws the magical bow,
> I would go to set my sorrow aloud.

(*Speaking.*) Where does that sound of playing come from ? It is the sound of the bow of Adzusa !

MIKO

Though I went to the door of the square building, Adzumaya——

APPARITION

——you thought no one came to knock.

AWOI NO UYE

Miko

How strange ! It is a lady of high rank whom I do not know. She comes in a broken carriage, a green wife clings to the shaft. She weeps. Is it——

Daijin

Yes, I think I know who it is. (*To the Apparition.*) I ask you to tell me your name.

Apparition

In the world of the swift-moving lightning I have no servant or envoi, neither am I consumed with self-pity. I came aimlessly hither, drawn only by the sound of the bow. Who do you think I am ? I am the spirit of the Princess Rokujo,[1] and when I was still in the world, spring was there with me. I feasted upon the cloud with the Sennin,[2] they shared in my feast of flowers. And on the Evening of Maple Leaves I had the moon for a mirror. I was drunk with colour and perfume. And for all my gay flare at that time I am now like a shut Morning-glory, awaiting the sunshine. And now I am come for a whim, I am come uncounting the hour, seizing upon no set

[1] As in Western folk-lore, demons often appear first in some splendid disguise.
[2] Spirits not unlike the Irish " Sidhe."

moment. I would set my sorrow aside. Let some one else bear it awhile.

CHORUS

Love turns back toward the lover, unkindness brings evil return. It is for no good deed or good purpose that you bring back a sorrow among us, our sorrows mount up without end.

APPARITION

The woman is hateful! I cannot keep back my blows. [*She strikes.*

MIKO

No. You are a princess of Rokujo! How can you do such things? Give over. Give over.

APPARITION

I cannot. However much you might pray. (*Reflectively, as if detached from her action, and describing it.*) So she went toward the pillow, and struck. Struck.

MIKO

Then standing up——

APPARITION

This hate is only repayment

AWOI NO UYE

MIKO

The flame of jealousy——

APPARITION

—will turn on one's own hand and burn.

MIKO

Do you not know?

APPARITION

Know! This is a just revenge.

CHORUS

Hateful, heart full of hate,
Though you are full of tears
Because of others' dark hatred,
Your love for Genji
Will not be struck out
Like a fire-fly's flash in the dark.

APPARITION

I, like a bush——

CHORUS

—am a body that has no root.
I fade as dew from the leaf,
Partly for that cause I hate her,
My love cannot be restored . . .
Not even in a dream.

It is a gleam cast up from the past. I am full of longing. I would be off in the secret coach, and crush her shade with me.

DAIJIN

Help. Awoi no Uye is sinking. Can you find Kohijiri of Tokokawa?

KIOGEN

I will call him. I call him.

WAKI (KOHIJIRI)

Do you call me to a fit place for prayer? To the window of the nine wisdoms, to the cushion of the ten ranks, to a place full of holy waters, and where there is a clear moon?

KIOGEN

Yes, yes.

WAKI

How should I know? I do not go about in the world. You come from the Daijin. Wait. I am ready. I will come.

[*He crosses the stage or bridge.*

DAIJIN

I thank you for coming.

WAKI

Where is the patient?

AWOI NO UYE

DAIJIN

She is there on that bed.

WAKI

I will begin the exorcism at once.

DAIJIN

I thank you. Please do so.

WAKI
(beginning the ritual)

Then Gioja called upon En no Gioja, and
he hung about his shoulders a cloak that had
swept the dew of the seven jewels in climbing
the peaks of Tai Kou and of Kori in Riobu.
He wore the cassock of forbearance to keep
out unholy things. He took the beads of red
wood, the square beads with hard corners,
and whirling and striking said prayer. But
one prayer.

Namaku, Samanda, Basarada.

[*During this speech the* APPARITION *has
disappeared. That is, the first* SHITE,
the PRINCESS OF ROKUJO. *Her costume
was " The under kimono black satin,
tight from the knees down, embroidered
with small, irregular, infrequent circles
of flowers; the upper part, stiff gold*

203

'NOH'

brocade, just shot through with purples,
greens, and reds."
[*The* HANNYA *has come on.   Clothed in a
scarlet hakama, white upper dress, and
" The terrible mask with golden eyes."
She has held a white scarf over her
head.   She looks up.   Here follows the
great dance climax of the play.*

HANNYA
(*threatening*)

Oh, Gioja, turn back !   Turn back, or you
rue it.

WAKI

Let whatever evil spirit is here bow before
Gioja, and know that Gioja will drive it out.
[*He continues whirling the rosary.*

CHORUS
(*invoking the powerful good spirits*)
On the east stand Gosanze Miowo.

HANNYA
(*opposing other great spirits*)
On the south stand Gundari Yasha.

CHORUS
On the west stand Dai Itoku Miowo.

AWOI NO UYE

HANNYA

On the north stand Kongo——

CHORUS

——Yasha Miowo.

HANNYA

In the middle Dai Sei——

CHORUS

Fudo Miowo
Namaku Samanda Basarada !
Senda Makaroshana Sowataya
Wun tarata Kamman,
Choga Sessha Tokudai Chiye
Chiga Shinja Sokushin Jobutsu.

HANNYA
(overcome by the exorcism)

O terrible names of the spirits. This is my last time. I cannot return here again.

CHORUS

By hearing the scripture the evil spirit is melted. Bosatsu came hither, his face was full of forbearance and pity. Pity has melted her heart, and she has gone into Buddha. Thanksgiving.

FINIS

KAKITSUBATA

By Motokiyo

EITHER Motokiyo or Fenollosa seems to have thought that the old sage Narihira was in his day the incarnation of a certain Bosatsu or high spirit. Secondly, that the music of this spirit was known and was called " Kohi " or " Gobusaki's " music. Narihira seems, after favour, to have been exiled from the court, and to have written poems of regret.

In the play a certain priest, given to melancholy, and with a kindliness for the people of old stories, meets with the spirit of one of Narihira's ladies who has identified herself with the Iris, that is to say, the flowers are the thoughts or the body of her spirit.

She tells him of her past and of Narihira's, and how the music of Gobusaki will lift a man's soul into paradise. She then returns to her heaven.

'NOH'

The rest is, I hope, apparent in the play as I have set it.

CHARACTERS

The Scene is in Mikawa

SPIRIT OF THE IRIS, KAKITSUBATA.
A PRIEST.
CHORUS.

PRIEST

I am a priest who travels to see the sights in many provinces; I have been to Miyako city and seen all the ward shrines and places of interest; I will now push on to the east country. Every night it is a new bed and the old urge of sorrow within me. I have gone by Mino and Owari without stopping, and I am come to Mikawa province to see the flowers of Kakitsubata in the height of their full season. Now the low land is before me, I must go down and peer closely upon them.
Time does not stop and spring passes,
The lightfoot summer comes nigh us,
The branching trees and the bright unmindful
    grass
Do not forget their time,
They take no thought, yet remember
To show forth their colour in season.

KAKITSUBATA

SPIRIT

What are you doing here in this swamp?

PRIEST

I am a priest on my travels. I think these very fine iris. What place is this I am come to?

SPIRIT

Eight Bridges, Yatsubashi of Mikawa, an iris plantation. You have the best flowers before you, those of the deepest colour, as you would see if you had any power of feeling.

PRIEST

I can see it quite well; they are, I think, the Kakitsubata iris that are set in an ancient legend. Can you tell me who wrote down the words?

SPIRIT

In the Ise Monogatari you read, " By the eight bridges, by the web of the crossing waters in Kumode, the iris come to the full, they flaunt there and scatter their petals." And when some one laid a wager with Narihira he made an acrostic which says, " These flowers brought their court dress from China."

PRIEST

Then Narihira came hither? From the far end of Adzuma?

'NOH'

SPIRIT

Here? Yes. And every other place in the north, the deep north.

PRIEST

Though he went through many a province, what place was nearest his heart?

SPIRIT

This place, Yatsubashi.

PRIEST

Here with the wide-petalled iris
On the lowlands of Mikawa.

SPIRIT

Throughout the length and width of his journeys——

PRIEST

Their colour was alive in his thought.

SPIRIT

He was Narihira of old, the man of the stories.

PRIEST

Yet this iris. . . .

SPIRIT
(*still standing by the pillar and bending sideways*)

These very flowers before you——

KAKITSUBATA

Chorus

—are not the thing of importance. She
would say :
" The water by the shore is not shallow.
The man who bound himself to me
Returned times out of mind in his thought
To me and this cobweb of waters."
It was in this fashion he knew her, when
he was strange in this place.

Spirit

I should speak.

Priest

What is it ?

Spirit

Though this is a very poor place, will you
pass the night in my cottage ?

Priest

Most gladly.   I will come after a little.

----

*[Up to this point the spirit has appeared
as a simple young girl of the locality.
She now leaves her pillar and goes off
to the other side of the stage to be
dressed.   She returns in her true
appearance, that is, as the great lady*

beloved of old by Narihira. She wears
a black hoshiben crest or hat, an over-
dress of gauze, purple with golden
flowers, an underdress of glaring orange
with green and gold pattern. This
shows only a little beneath the great
enveloping gauze.

SPIRIT
(to tire-women)

No, no. This hat, this ceremonial gown,
the Chinese silk, Karaginu, . . . Look !

PRIEST

How strange. In that tumble-down cottage ;
in the bower, a lady clad in bright robes !   In
the pierced hat of Sukibitai's time.   She seems
to speak, saying, " Behold me ! "
What can all this mean ?

KAKITSUBATA

This is the very dress brought from China,
Whereof they sing in the ballad,
'Tis the gown of the Empress Takago,
Queen of old to Seiwa Tenno,[1]
She is Narihira's beloved,
Who danced the Gosetsu music.

[1] Emperor of Japan, A.D. 859-876.

KAKITSUBATA

At eighteen she won him,
She was his light in her youth.

This hat is for Gosetsu dancing,
For the Dance of Toyo no Akari.
Narihira went covered in like.
A hat and a robe of remembrance !
I am come clothed in a memory.

Priest
You had better put them aside. But who
are you ?

The Lady
I am indeed the spirit, Kakitsubata, the
colours of remembrance.

And Narihira was the incarnation of the
Bosatsu of Gokusaki's music. Holy magic is
run through his words and through the notes
of his singing, till even the grass and the flowers
pray to him for the blessings of dew.

Priest
A fine thing in a world run waste,
To the plants that are without mind,
I preach the law of Bosatsu.

Lady
This was our service to Buddha,
This dance, in the old days.

'NOH'

PRIEST
(hearing the music)
This is indeed spirit music.

LADY
He took the form of a man.

PRIEST
Journeying out afar
From his bright city.

LADY
Saving all——

PRIEST
——by his favour.

CHORUS
Going out afar and afar
I put on robes for the dance.

LADY
A robe for the sorrow of parting.

CHORUS
I send the sleeves back to the city.

LADY
This story has no beginning and no end,
No man has known the doer and no man has
   seen the deed.

KAKITSUBATA

In the old days a man
Wearing his first hat-of-manhood
Went out a-hunting
Toward the town of Kasuga in Nara.

CHORUS

We think it was in the time
Of the reign of Nimmio Tenno.

He was granted by Imperial Decree
Reading : " About the beginning of March,
When the mists are still banked upon Ouchi-
    yama the mountain. . . ."
He was granted the hat-insignia, sukibitai,
As chief messenger to the festival of Kasuga.

LADY

An unusual favour.

CHORUS

It was a rare thing to hold the plays and
Genbuku ceremony in the palace itself. This
was the first time it had happened.
The world's glory is only for once,
Comes once, blows once, and soon fades,
So also to him : he went out
To seek his luck in Adzuma,
Wandering like a piece of cloud, at last
After years he came

215

And looking upon the waves at Ise and Owari,
He longed for his brief year of glory :
        The waves, the breakers return,
        But my glory comes not again,
                Narihira, Narihira,
        My glory comes not again.
    He stood at the foot of Asama of Shinano,
and saw the smoke curling upwards.

LADY

The smoke is now curling up
From the peak of Asama.
                Narihira, Narihira,
        My glory comes not again.

CHORUS

Strangers from afar and afar,
Will they not wonder at this ?
He went on afar and afar
And came to Mikawa, the province,
To the flowers Kakitsubata
That flare and flaunt in their marsh
By the many-bridged cobweb of waters.
    " She whom I left in the city ? " thought
Narihira. But in the long tale, Monogatari,
there is many a page full of travels . . . and
yet at the place of eight bridges the stream-
bed is never dry.

KAKITSUBATA

He was pledged with many a lady.
The fire-flies drift away
From the jewelled blind,
Scattering their little lights
And then flying and flying :

Souls of fine ladies
Going up into heaven.

And here in the under-world
The autumn winds come blowing and blow-
ing,
And the wild ducks cry : " Kari ! . . . Kari !"

I who speak, an unsteady wraith,
A form impermanent, drifting after this fashion,
Am come to enlighten these people.
Whether they know me I know not.

SPIRIT
A light that does not lead on to darkness.

CHORUS
(*singing the poem of Narihira's*)
No moon !
The spring
Is not the spring of the old days,
My body
Is not my body,

But only a body grown old.
        Narihira, Narihira,
     My glory comes not again.

CHORUS

Know then that Narihira of old made these verses for the Queen of Seiwa Tenno. The body unravels its shred, the true image divides into shade and light. Narihira knew me in the old days. Doubt it not, stranger. And now I begin my dance, wearing the ancient bright mantle.

[Dance and its descriptions.

SPIRIT

The flitting snow before the flowers :
The butterfly flying.

CHORUS

The nightingales fly in the willow tree :
The pieces of gold flying.

SPIRIT

The iris Kakitsubata of the old days
Is planted anew.

CHORUS

With the old bright colour renewed.

KAKITSUBATA

SPIRIT

Thus runs each tale from its beginning,
We wear the bright iris crest of Azame.

CHORUS

What are the colours of the iris ?
Are they like one another, the flower,
Kakitsubata, Ayame.
> [*The grey and olive robed chorus obscure
> the bright dancer.*

What is that that cries from the tree ?
> [*The spirit is going away, leaving its
> apparition, which fades as it returns
> to the aether.*

SPIRIT

It is only the cracked husk of the locust.

CHORUS

(closing the play)

The sleeves are white like the snow of the
    Uno Flower
Dropping their petals in April.
Day comes, the purple flower
  Opens its heart of wisdom,
It fades out of sight by its thought.
The flower soul melts into Buddha.

'NOH'

Note

I have left one or two points of this play
unexplained in the opening notice. I do not
think any one will understand the beauty of
it until he has read it twice. The emotional
tone is perhaps apparent. The spirit manifests
itself in that particular iris marsh because
Narihira in passing that place centuries before
had thought of her. Our own art is so
much an art of emphasis, and even of over-
emphasis, that it is difficult to consider the
possibilities of an absolutely unemphasized art,
an art where the author trusts so implicitly
that his auditor will know what things are
profound and important.

The Muses were " the Daughters of
Memory." It is by memory that this spirit
appears, she is able or " bound " because of
the passing thought of these iris. That is to
say, they, as well as the first shadowy and
then bright apparition, are the outer veils of
her being. Beauty is the road to salvation,
and her apparition " to win people to the
Lord " or " to enlighten these people " is part
of the ritual, that is to say, she demonstrates
the " immortality of the soul " or the " per-
manence or endurance of the individual per-

KAKITSUBATA

sonality " by her apparition—first, as a simple girl of the locality; secondly, in the ancient splendours. At least that is the general meaning of the play so far as I understand it.

E. P.

CHORIO

By Nobumitsu (who died in the 13th year of Yeisho, A.D. 1516)

CHARACTERS

The Scene is in China

FIRST SHITE, an old man.
SECOND SHITE, KOSEKKO.
WAKI, CHORIO.

PART I

WAKI

I am Chorio,[1] a subject of Koso of Kan, though I am busy in service I had a strange dream that there was in Kahi an earthen bridge, and that as I leaned on the bridge-rail there came an old man on horseback. And he dropped one of his shoes and bade me pick

[1] Chinese. Chang Liang died 187 B.C. Koso of Kan = Kao Tsu, first Emperor of the Han dynasty. Kahi = Hsia-p'ei, in the north of Kiangsu. Kosekko = Huang Shih Kung, Yellow Stone Duke.

up the shoe. I thought this uncivil, yet he seemed so uncommon a figure and so gone on in old age that I went and picked up the shoe. "You've a true heart," he said, "come back here in five days' time, and I will teach you all there is to know about fighting."

He said that, and then I woke up, and now it's five days since the dream, and I am on my way to Kahi.

Dawn begins to show in the sky. I am afraid I may be too late. The mountain is already lit, and I am just reaching the bridge.

SHITE

Chorio, you are late, you have not kept your promise. I came quite early, and now it is much too late. Hear the bell there.

CHORUS

Too late now. Come again. Come in five days' time if you carry a true heart within you. And I shall be here, and will teach you the true craft of fighting. Keep the hour, and keep true to your promise. How angry the old man seemed. How suddenly he is gone. Chorio, see that you come here in time.

CHORIO

Chorio

He is angry. I am sorry. Why do I follow
a man wholly a stranger? Foolish. Yet, if he
would teach me his secrets of strategy. . . .

Chorus

I think that he will come back. He does
not like wasting his time. Still, he will come
back again. See, he has gone away happy.

PART II

Chorio

" Frost tinges the jasper terrace,
A fine stork, a black stork sings in the heaven,
Autumn is deep in the valley of Hako,
The sad monkeys cry out in the midnight,
The mountain pathway is lonely."

Chorus

The morning moonlight lies over the world
And flows through the gap of these mountains,
White frost is on Kahi bridge, the crisp water
    wrinkles beneath it,
There is no print in the frost on the bridge,
No one has been by this morning.
Chorio, that is your luck. That shadow shows
    a man urging his horse.

'NOH'

Old Man

I am the old man, Kosekko.   Since Chorio
is loyal in service, no fool, ready at learning . . .

Chorus

Since he cares so much for the people . . .

Kosekko

His heart has been seen in high heaven.

Chorus

The Boddisatwa are ready to bless him.

Kosekko

I will teach him the secrets of battle.

Chorus

He says he will teach Chorio to conquer
the enemy, and to rule well over the people.
He urges his horse, and seeing this from far
off, seeing the old man so changed in aspect,
with eye gleaming out and with such dignity
in his bearing, Chorio has knelt down on the
bridge awaiting Kosekko.

Kosekko

Chorio, you are come in good time.   Come
nearer and listen.

226

CHORIO

CHORIO

Chorio then stood up and smoothed out his hat and his robe.

KOSEKKO

I know quite well he is wise, but still I will try him.

CHORUS

Kosekko kicked off his shoe so it fell in the river. Then Chorio leapt in for the shoe, but the river flowed between rocks ; it was full of currents and arrow-like rapids. He went diving and floating and still not reaching the shoe.[1]

See how the waves draw back. A thick mist covers the place, a dragon moves in darkness, ramping among the waves, lolling its fiery tongue. It is fighting with Chorio ; see, it has seized on the shoe.

CHORIO

Chorio drew his sword calmly.

CHORUS

He struck a great blow at the dragon ; there was terrible light on his sword. See, the dragon draws back and leaves Chorio with

[1] One must consider this as dance motif.

the shoe. Then Chorio sheathed his sword
and brought up the shoe to Kosekko, and
buckled it fast to his foot.

Kosekko

And Kosekko got down from his horse.

Chorus

He alighted, saying, "Well done. Well
done." And he gave a scroll of writing to
Chorio, containing all the secret traditions of
warfare. And Kosekko said, "That dragon
was Kwannon. She came here to try your
heart, and she must be your goddess hereafter."

Then the dragon went up to the clouds,
and Kosekko drew back to the highest peak,
and set his light in the sky ; was changed to
the yellow stone.

FINIS

GENJO

By Kongo

Story from Utai Kimmō Zuye

In China, under the Tō dynasty (A.D. 604–927), there was a biwa player named Renjōbu, and he had a biwa called Genjō. In the reign of Nimmyō Tennō (A.D. 834–850) Kamon no Kami Sadatoshi met Renjōbu in China, and learnt from him three tunes, Ryūsen (The Flowing Fountain), Takuboku[1] (The Woodpecker), and the tune Yōshin. He also brought back to our court the biwa named Genjō.

[1] The words of " Takuboku " are—

> In the South Hill there's a bird
> That calls itself the woodpecker.
> When it's hungry, it eats its tree ;
> When it's tired, it rests in the boughs.
>
> Don't mind about other people ;
> Just make up your mind what you want.
> If you're pure, you'll get honour ;
> If you're foul, you'll get shame.
>   By Lady Tso, A.D. 4th cent.

' NOH '

Murakami Tennō (947–967) was a great biwa player. One moonlit night, when he was sitting alone in the Southern Palace, he took the biwa Genjō and sang the old song :

> Slowly the night draws on
> And the dew on the grasses deepens.
> Long after man's heart is at rest
> Clouds trouble the moon's face—
> Through the long night till dawn.

Suddenly the spirit of Renjōbu appeared to him and taught him two new tunes, Jōgen and Sekishō (the Stone Image). These two, with the three that Sadatoshi had brought before, became the Five Biwa Tunes.

These five tunes were transmitted to Daijō Daijin Moronaga, who was the most skilful player in the Empire.

Moronaga purposed to take the biwa Genjō and go with it to China in order to perfect his knowledge. But on the way the spirit of Murakami Tennō appeared to him at Suma under the guise of an old salt-burner.[1]

[1] Note supplied by A. D. W.

GENJO

GENJO

PART I

The Scene is in Settsu

CHARACTERS

FIRST SHITE, an old man.
TSURE, an old woman.
TSURE, Fujiwara no Moronaga.
SECOND SHITE, the Emperor Murakami.
TSURE, Riujin, the Dragon God.
WAKI, an attendant of Moronaga.

WAKI

What road will get us to Mirokoshi,[1] far in
the eight-folded waves?

MORONAGA

I am the Daijo Daijin Moronaga.

WAKI

He is my master, and the famous master of
the biwa, and he wishes to go to China to
study more about music, but now he is turning
aside from the straight road to see the moonlight in Suma and Tsu-no-Kuni.[2]

---

[1] China.
[2] Tsu-no-Kuni is the poetical name for Settsu province.

231

'NOH'

Moronaga

When shall I see the sky-line of Miyako,
the capital? We started at midnight. Yama-
zaki is already behind us.

Waki

Here is Minato river and the wood of
Ikuta; the moon shows between the black
trees, a lonely track. But I am glad to be
going to Mirokoshi. The forest of Koma is
already behind us. Now we are coming to
Suma.

Now we have come to the sea-board, Suma
in Tsu-no-Kuni. Let us rest here a while
and ask questions.

Old Man and Old Woman

It's a shabby life, lugging great salt tubs,
and yet the shore is so lovely that one puts off
one's sorrow, forgets it.

Old Man

The setting sun floats on the water.

Old Man and Old Woman

Even the fishermen know something grown
out of the place, and speak well of their sea-
coast.

GENJO

OLD WOMAN

The isles of Kii show through the cloud to the southward.

OLD MAN

You can see the ships there, coming through the gateway of Yura.

OLD WOMAN

And the pine-trees, as far off as Sumiyoshi.

OLD MAN

And the cottages at Tojima, Koya, and Naniwa.

OLD WOMAN

They call it the island of pictures.

OLD MAN

Yet no one is able to paint it.

OLD MAN AND OLD WOMAN

Truly a place full of charms.

CHORUS

The air of this place sets one thinking. Awaji, the sea, a place of fishermen, see now their boats will come in. The rain crouches low in the cloud. Lift up your salt tubs, Aie! It's a long tramp, heavy working. Carry

233

along, from Ise Island to the shore of Akogi.
There is no end to this business. The salt at
Tango is worse. Now we go down to Suma.
A dreary time at this labour. No one knows
aught about us. Will any one ask our trouble?

OLD MAN

I will go back to the cottage and rest.

WAKI

(*at the cottage door*)
Is any one home here? We are looking for
lodging.

OLD MAN

I am the man of the place.

WAKI

This is the great Daijin Moronaga, the
master of biwa, on his way to far Mirokoshi.
May we rest here?

OLD MAN

Please take him somewhere else.

WAKI

What! you won't give us lodging. Please
let us stay here.

GENJO

OLD MAN

The place isn't good enough, but you may come in if you like.

OLD WOMAN

When they were praying for rain in the garden of Shin-sen (Divine Fountain), he drew secret music from the strings of his biwa——

OLD MAN

—and the dragon-god seemed to like it. The clouds grew out of the hard sky of a sudden, and the rain fell and continued to fall. And they have called him Lord of the Rain.

OLD WOMAN

If you lodge such a noble person——

OLD MAN

—I might hear his excellent playing.

BOTH

It will be a night worth remembering.

CHORUS

The bard Semimaru played upon his biwa at the small house in Osaka, now a prince will play in the fisherman's cottage. A rare night.

'NOH'

Let us wait here in Suma. The pine-wood shuts out the wind and the bamboo helps to make stillness. Only the little ripple of waves sounds from a distance. They will not let you sleep for a while. Play your biwa. We listen.

WAKI

I will ask him to play all night.

MORONAGA

Maybe it was spring when Genji was exiled and came here into Suma, and had his first draught of sorrow, of all the sorrows that come to us. And yet his travelling clothes were not dyed in tears. Weeping, he took out his small lute, and thought that the shore wind had in it a cry like his longing, and came to him from far cities.

CHORUS

That was the sound of the small lute and the shore wind sounding together, but this biwa that we will hear is the rain walking in showers. It beats on the roof of the cottage. We cannot sleep for the rain. It is interrupting the music.

OLD MAN

Why do you stop your music?

GENJO

WAKI

He stopped because of the rain.

OLD MAN

Yes, it is raining. We will put our straw mats on the roof.

OLD WOMAN

Why?

OLD MAN

They will stop the noise of the rain, and we can go on hearing his music.

BOTH

So they covered the wooden roof.

CHORUS

And they came back and sat close to hear him.

WAKI

Why have you put the mats on the roof.

OLD MAN

The rain sounded out of the key. The biwa sounds " yellow bell," and the rain gives a " plate " note. Now we hear only the " bell."

CHORUS

We knew you were no ordinary person. Come, play the biwa yourself.

'NOH'

Old Man and Old Woman
The waves at this side of the beach can play their own biwa; we did not expect to be asked.

Chorus
Still they were given the biwa.

Old Man
The old man pulled at the strings.

Old Woman
The old woman steadied the biwa.

Chorus
A sound of pulling and plucking, " Barari, karari, karari, barari," a beauty filled full of tears, a singing bound in with the music, unending, returning.

Moronaga
Moronaga thought——

Chorus
—I learned in Hi-no-Moto all that men knew of the biwa, and now I am ashamed to have thought of going to China. I need not go out of this country. So he secretly went out of the cottage. And the old man, not

GENJO

knowing, went on playing the biwa, and singing
" Etenraku," the upper cloud music, this
    song :
" The nightingale nests in the plum tree, but
    what will she do with the wind ?
Let the nightingale keep to her flowers."
    The old man is playing, not knowing the
guest has gone out.

Old Woman
The stranger has gone.

Old Man
What ! he is gone. Why didn't you stop
him ?

Both
So they both ran after the stranger.

Chorus
And taking him by the sleeve, they said,
" The night is still only half over.   Stay here."

Moronaga
Why do you stop me ? I am going back
to the capital now, but later I will return.
Who are you ? What are your names ?

'NOH'

Both

Emperor Murakami, and the lady is Nashitsubo.

Chorus

To stop you from going to China we looked on you in a dream, by the sea-coasts at Suma. So saying, they vanished.

PART II

The Emperor Murakami

I came up to the throne in the sacred era of Gengi,[1] when the fine music came from Mirokoshi, the secret and sacred music, and the lutes Genjo, Seizan,[2] and Shishimaru. The last brought from the dragon world. And now I will play on it.

And he looked out at the sea and called on the dragon god, and played on " Shishimaru."

The lion-dragon floated out of the waves, and the eight goddesses of the dragon stood with him, and he then gave Moronaga the biwa. And Moronaga took it, beginning to play. And the dragon king moved with the

---

[1] A.D. 901-923.

[2] The lute Seizan. See first speech of " Tsunemasa."

GENJO

music, and the waves beat with drum rhythm. And Murakami took up one part. That was music. Then Murakami stepped into the cloudy chariot, drawn by the eight goddesses of the dragon, and was lifted up beyond sight. And Moronaga took a swift horse back to his city, bearing that biwa with him.

FINIS

APPENDICES

APPENDIX I

Shunkwan, by Motokiyo (b. 1374, d. 1455).

Plot.—When Kiyomori [1] was at the height of his power three men plotted against him. They were detected and exiled to Devil's Island ; " for many years they knew the spring only by the green new grass, and autumn by the turning of the leaves."

Then when Kiyomori's daughter was about to give birth to a child, many prisoners and exiles were pardoned in order to propitiate the gods, and among them Shunkwan's companions, but not the chief conspirator Shunkwan.

On the ninth day of the ninth month, which day is called " Choyo " and is considered very lucky, because Hosō of China drank ceremonial wine on that day and lived 7000 years, the two exiled companions of Shunkwan are performing service to their god Kumano Gongen. They have no white prayer cord, and must use the white cord of their exile's dress ; they have no white rice to scatter, and so they scatter white sand. With this scene

[1] Kiyomori, 1118–81.

245

the Noh opens. Shunkwan, who alone is a priest, enters, and should offer a cup of saké, as in the proper service for receiving pilgrims, but he has only a cup of water.

While this ceremony is in progress, the imperial messengers arrive with the emperor's writ ; they pronounce the names of Yasuyori and Naritsune, but not Shunkwan's. He thinks there must be some error. He seizes the paper and reads, and is frenzied with grief. He tries to detain his companions, but the messengers hurry them off. Shunkwan seizes the boat's cable. The messenger cuts it. Shunkwan falls to earth, and the others go off, leaving him alone.

This is, of course, not a " play " in our sense. It is a programme for a tremendous dance.

Modus of Presentation (Asakusa, October 30, 1898).—The companions wear dull blue and brown. Shunkwan's mask is of a dead colour, full of wrinkles, with sunken cheeks and eyes. His costume is also of blue and brown. The finest singing and dancing are after the others have entered the boat. Everything is concentrated on the impression of a feeling.

The scene is in " an island of Stasuma."

Koi no Omoni (" The Burden of Love "), said to be by the Emperor Gohanazono (1429–65).

Plot.—Yamashina Shoshi was the emperor's gardener, and as the court ladies were always walking about in the garden, he fell in love with one of them. He wished to keep this secret, but in some way it became known. Then a court officer said to him, " If you can carry this light and richly brocaded burden on your back, and carry it many thousand times round the garden, you will win the lady you love." But for all its seeming so light and being so finely ornamented, it was a very heavy load, and whenever he tried to lift it he fell to the ground, and he sang and complained of it, and at last he died trying to lift it.

And the court officer told the lady, and she was filled with pity and sang a short and beautiful song, and the ghost of Shoshi came and sang to her of the pain he had in this life, reproaching her for her coldness.

Modus.—From the very first the burden of love lay in the centre front of the stage, thus " becoming actually one of the characters." It was a cube done up in red and gold brocade and tied with green cords. The hero wore a mask, which seemed unnecessarily old, ugly, and wrinkled. His costume subdued, but rich. The court lady gorgeously dressed, with smiling young girl's mask and glittering pendant, East-Indian sort of head-dress.

The lady sat at the right corner, immobile, rather the lover's image of his mistress than a living being. He sings, complains, and tries several times to lift the burden, but cannot. The court officer sits a little toward the right-back. Shoshi dies and passes out.

The officer addresses the lady, who suddenly

seems to come to life. She listens, then leaves her seat, half-kneels near the burden, her face set silently and immovably toward it. This is more graphic and impressive than can well be imagined. All leave the stage save this silent figure contemplating the burden.

The Shoshi's ghost comes in, covered with glittering superb brocades, he uses a crutch, has a mane of flying grey hair, and a face that looks like an " elemental."

KANAWA, THE IRON RING, by Motokiyo.

Story.—In the reign of Saga Tenno there was a princess who loved unavailingly, and she became so enraged with jealousy that she went to the shrine of Kibune and prayed for seven days that she might become a hannya. On the seventh day the god had pity, and appeared to her and said, " If you wish to become a hannya go to the Uji river and stay twenty-five days in the water." And she returned rejoicing to Kioto, and parted her hair into five strands and painted her face and her body red, and put an iron ring on her head with three candles in it. And she took in her mouth a double fire-stick, burning at both ends. And when she walked out in the streets at night people thought her a devil.

From this it happens that when Japanese women are jealous they sometimes go to a temple at night wearing an iron ring (Kanawa) with candles in it. Sometimes they use also a straw doll in the incantation.

APPENDIX I

Modus.—First comes Kiogen, the farce character, and says he has had a god-dream, and that he will tell it to the woman who is coming to pray.

Then comes the woman. Kiogen asks if she comes every night. He tells her his dream, and how she is to become a hannya by the use of Kanawa. She goes. Her face changes en route. Enter the faithless husband, who says he lives in Shimokio, the Lower City, and has been having very bad dreams. He goes to the priest Abē, who tells him that a woman's jealousy is at the root of it, and that his life is in danger that very night. The husband confesses his infidelity. The priest starts a counter exorcism, using a life-sized straw doll with the names of both husband and wife put inside it. He uses the triple takadana[1] and five coloured " gohei," red, blue, yellow, black, white. Storm comes with thunder and lightning. The woman appears. She and the chorus sing, interrupting each other— she complaining, the chorus interpreting her thoughts. She approaches her husband's pillow with the intention of killing him. But the power of the exorcism prevails, and she vanishes into the air.

MATSUKAZE, by Kiyotsugu.

A wandering priest sees the ghost of the two fisher girls, Matsukaze and Murasame, still gathering salt on the seashore at Suma. They still seem to feel the waves washing over them, and say,

[1] Generally called mitegura ; see p. 114.

" Even the shadows of the moon are wet," " The autumn wind is full, full of thoughts, thoughts of the sea." They seem to wish to be back in their old hard life, and say the moon is " envious " of the ghost life, and will only shine on the living ; that the dews are gathered up by the sun, but that they lie like old grass left to rot on the sea-beach. " How beautiful is the evening at Suma for all the many times we have seen it and might be tired with seeing it. How faint are the fishermen's voices. We see the fisher boats in the offing. The faint moon is the only friend. Children sing under the field-sweeping wind; the wind is salt with the autumn. O how sublime is this night. I will go back to shore, for the tide is now at its full. We hang our wet sleeves over our shoulders, salt dripping from them. The waves rush to the shore, a stork sings in the reeds. The storm gathers in from all sides ; how shall we pass through this night. Cold night, clear moon, and we two in deep shadow."

APPENDIX II

FENOLLOSA's notes go into considerable detail as
to how one must place large jars under the proper
Noh stage for resonance : concerning the officials
in the ministry of music in the reign of some emperor or other; concerning musical instruments,
etc.; concerning special ceremonies, etc. A part
of this material can, I think, be of interest only
to scholars; at least I am not prepared to edit it
until I know how much or how little general interest
there is in the Japanese drama and its methods
of presentation. Many facts might be extremely
interesting if one had enough knowledge of Noh,
and could tell where to fit them in. Many names
might be rich in association, which are, at the
present stage of our knowledge, a rather dry
catalogue.

Still, I may be permitted a very brief summary
of a section of notes based, I think, on a long work
by Professor Ko-haka-mura.

Certain instruments are very old (unless we have
pictures of all these instruments, a list of Japanese
names with the approximate dates of their invention
will convey little to us). Music is divided roughly

251

into what comes from China, from Korea, and what is native. "Long and short songs, which sang out the heart of the people, were naturally rhythmic." Foreign music . . . various schools and revolutions . . . priests singing in harmony (?) with the biwa. Puppet plays (about 1596, I think, unless the date 1184 higher on the page is supposed to be connected with "the great genius Chikamatsu"). Chikamatsu, author of 97 jōruri plays, lived 1653–1724. Various forms of dancing, female dancing, "turning piece," some forms of female dancing forbidden. Music for funerals and ceremonies.

"The thoughts of men, when they are only uttered as they are, are called 'tada goto,' plain word. But when they are too deep for 'plain word' we make 'pattern decoration' (aya), and have fushi (tones) for it."

An emperor makes the first koto from "decayed" wood; the sound of it was very clear and was heard from afar.

Field dances, shield dances, etc. "In the ninth month of the fourteenth year of Temmu (A.D. 686), the imperial order said: 'The male singers and female flute blowers must make it their own profession, and hand it down to their descendants and make them learn.' Hence these hereditary professions."

"In the festival of Toka, court ladies performed female dancing, ceremony of archery, wrestling (so the note seems to read). In the Buddhist service only foreign music was used."

APPENDIX II

More regulations for court ceremonies, not unlike the general meticulousness of "Leviticus."

Buddhism, growing popularity of Chinese music. "In Daijosai, the coronation festival, it was not the custom to use Chinese music. But in this ceremony at Nimmio Tenno's coronation, on the day of the dinner-party, they collected pebbles before the temple, planted new trees, spread sheets on the ground, scattered grain to represent the seashore, and took out boats upon it, and a dance was performed imitating fishermen picking up seaweed.

In the festival of the ninth month, literary men offered Chinese poems, so it may be that the music was also in Chinese style.

In the time of Genkio (1321–23), mention of a troupe of 140 dancers.

Udzumusa Masena (?) gives a list of pieces of music brought over from China. "Sansai Zuye," an old Japanese encyclopedia, certainly gives this list. Some of these names may be interesting as our knowledge of Noh increases. At any rate, I find already a few known names, notably the sea-wave dance mentioned in the Genji play already translated. I therefore give a partial list, which the reader may skip at his pleasure:

Brandish dancing, breaking camp music, virtue of war, whirling circle music, spring nightingale singing, heaven head jewel life, long life, jewel tree, back-garden flower (composed by a princess of China), King of Rakio (who always wore a mask on his face when he went into battle), congratulation

253

temple, 10,000 years (Banzai), black-head music, Kan province, five customs, courtesy and justice music, five saints' music, pleasant spring, pleasant heart, playing temple, red-white peach pear flower, autumn wind, Rindai (a place in the out-of-the-way country of To), green sea-waves (sei kai ha), plucking mulberry old man, King of Jin breaking camp, divine merit, great settling great peace, returning castle music, turning cup, congratulation king benevolence. Three pieces for sword-dancing : great peace, general music, the palace of Komon ; beating ball, music of (?) Ringin Koku. " A wild duck curving her foot is the dancing of Bosatsu mai." Kariobinga bird,[1] barbaric drinking wine, dinner drinking, " Inyang "[2] castle peace. Music of Tenjiku,[3] in which the dancers are masked to look like sparrows, scattering hands, pluck off head, Princess of So, perfumed leaves, 10,000 autumns' music.

[1] The Kariobinga bird belongs to the Gyokuraku Jōdo or Paradise of Extreme Felicity. The name is Sanskrit, the thing Indian.

[2] The name Inyang is wrong, but I cannot find the correct name.

[3] Tenjiku = India.

APPENDIX III

(From another talk with Umewaka Minoru)

THE clothes are put away in tansos (?), the costly ones on sliding boards, only a few at a time. Ordinary ones are draped in nagmochi (oblong chests). The best ones are easily injured, threads break, holes come, etc.

Costumes are not classified by the names of the rôles, but by the kind of cloth or by cut or their historic period, and if there are too many of each sort, by colour, or the various shape of the ornamental patterns. The best are only used for royal performances. The costume for Kakitsubata is the most expensive, one of these recently (i.e. 1901) cost over 500 yen. (*Note.*—I think they are now more expensive.—E. P.)

One does not always use the same combination of costumes ; various combinations of quiet costumes are permitted. His sons lay out a lot of costumes on the floor, and Umewaka makes a selection or a new colour scheme as he pleases. This does not take very long.

All his costumes were made before Isshin, and he will not have new ones. When the daimios sold their costumes after the revolution, he might have bought the most splendid, but he was poor. He saved a few in his own house. He collected what he could afford from second-hand shops. Many went abroad. He sold his own clothes and furniture to buy masks. Only Mayeda of Kashu kept his masks and costumes.

Varia. — The notations for singing are very difficult. Takasago is the most correct piece. If a student sings with another who sings badly, his own style is ruined.

Umewaka's struggles to start Noh again after the downfall of the old regime seem to have been long and complicated. Fenollosa has recorded them with considerable detail, but without very great clarity. This much seems to be certain, that without Umewaka's persistence through successive struggles and harassing disappointments, the whole or a great part of the art might have been lost.

APPENDIX IV

AN ATTEMPT TO RECORD SOME OF THE MUSIC OF HAGOROMO

THE following music is Fenollosa's transcription of the air for the lyric parts of Hagoromo. I doubt whether the Noh music can be rendered intelligibly by our notation. I have had this play sung to me. I can see that Fenollosa has done some things correctly, but it seems to me that many things in the singing are wholly unindicated in his script. A phonograph record would be, I believe, the only efficient means of recording the Noh singing for us.

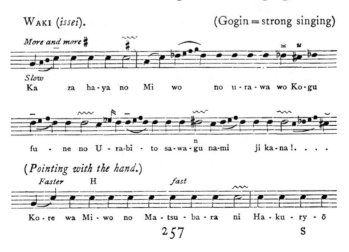

WAKI (*issei*). (Gogin = strong singing)

More and more

Slow
Ka   za ha‐ya no   Mi   wo   no u‐ra‐wa wo Ko‐gu

fu ‐ ne no U ‐ ra‐bi ‐ to sa‐wa‐gu na‐mi   ji ka‐na !. . . .

(*Pointing with the hand.*)
Faster   H   *fast*

Ko ‐ re   wa Mi ‐ wo no Ma ‐ tsu ‐ ba ‐ ra   ni   Ha ‐ ku ‐ ry ‐ ŏ

'NOH'

to mŏ - su giŏ - fu ni - te so - ro, Ban - ri no

Kŏ - zan ni ku - mo ta - chi ma - chi ni o - ko - ri, ...

i - chi rŏ no mei ge - tsu ni u - me ha - ji me - te ha - re - ri . .

Ge - ni na - do ka - na - ru to - ki shi - mo ya!

Ha, - ru no ke - shi - ki Ma - tsu - ba - ra no na - mi ta - chi

tsu - dzu - ku A - sa - ga - su - - mi. Tsu - ki mo no - ko - ri no

A - ma no ha - ra, O - yo - bi na - ki mi no na - ga - me - ni - mo

- - o. Ko - ko - ro so - ra na - ru ke - shi - ki Ka - na! . . .

Uta.

Wa - su - re - me ya Ya - ma - ji wo wa - ke - te Ki - yo - mi ga - ta

ha - ru - ka ni mi - wo no Ma - tsu - ba - ra ni ta - chi su - re

258

I - za ya ka - yo - wan, ta - chi su - re i - za - ya ka - yo - wan.

Ka - ze mu - ka - u Ku - mo no u - ki - na - mi ta - tsu - to

mi - te Ku - mo no u - ki - na - mi ta - tsu - to mi - te

tsu - ri se - de hi - to ya Ka - ye - ru - ran, Ma - te shi -

ba - shi ha - ru na - ra - ba fu - ku - mo no do - ke - ki a - sa -

ka - ze no Ma - tsu wa to - ki - wa no ko - ye dzo - ka - shi,

Na - mi wa o - to - na - ki A - sa - na - gi ni tsu - ri bi - to ō - ki

o - bu - ne ka - na. Tsu - ri bi - to ō - ki o - bu - ne ka - na!

CHORUS.
Slow

Na - mi - da no tsu - yu no ta - ma ka - dzu - ra

Ka - dza - shi no ha - na . . . mo Shi - wo shi - wo . . . to

'NOH'

Ten - nin no go su - i mo me no ma - ye ni

mi - ye - te a - sa - ma shi - ja . . . .

SHITE.

Slow

A-ma no ha - ra fu - ri sa - ke mi - re - ba Ka-su-mi ta - tsu

Ku - mo - ji ma - do - yi - te yu - ku ye shi - ra - dzu - mo.

CHORUS.

Slow

Su - mi na - re - shi So - ra ni i - tsu - shi - ka yu - ku ku - mo no

U - ra - ya - ma shi - ki Ke - shi - ki ka - na.

Ka - ryō bin - ga no na - re na - re shi,

Ka - ryō bin - ga no na - re na - re - shi,

Ko - ye i - ma sa - ra ni wa - dzu - ka na - ru,

Ka - ri ga ne no Ka - ye - ri yu - ku A - ma - ji wo

260

APPENDIX IV

ki · ke · ba na · tsu ka · shi ya . . . . .

Chi · do · ri Ka · mo me no o · ki · tsu na · mi

slow

Yu · ku ka Ka · ye · ru ka ha · ru · ka · ze no . .

So · ra ni fu · ku ma · de na · tsu ka · shi ya,

slow

So · ra ni fu · ku ma · de na · tsu ka · shi ya.

Slow dance.

CHORUS.

A · dzu · ma a · so · bi · no Su · ru · ga mai, A · dzu · ma a · so · bi ·

slower

no Su · ru · ga mai Ko · no to · ki ya . . ha · ji · me na · ru · ran

So · re . . hi · sa · ka · ta no . . . A · me to ip · pa

fast

Ni · jin shu · tsuse no i · ni · shui · ye

261

'NOH'

APPENDIX IV

Chorus.

Fast   *slower*

Tsu - ki no ka - tsu - ra no mi wo wa - ke - te . . .

slow

Ka - ri ni 'A - dzu - ma no . . Su - - - ru - ga mai . . .

fast

yo ni tsu - ta - ye . . ta - ru kio-ku to . . ka - - ya - a . .

Strong   *soft*

i - i - i - i - i - i - i - i.

Beginning.

1. Ha - ru - ğa - su - mi 1. ta - na - bi - ki ni ke - ri hi -

fast

sa - ka - ta - no 3. Tsu - ki - no . . ka - tsu - ra - no ha - na - ya - sa - ku

2. Ge - - - ni ha - na - ka - zu - ra i - ro - me - ku - wa

fast

ha - ru - no shi - ru - shi ka - ya 1. O - mo - shi - ro - ya

A - me - na - ra - de 1. Ko - ko - mo ta - ye - na - ri

263

'NOH'

APPENDIX IV

mi · su · ye · ni · te   Tsu · ki · mo · ku · mo · ra · nu   hi · no · mo · to · ya

SHITE.

Slow   *fast*

Ki · mi · ğa · yo · wa   A · ma · no   ha · go · ro · mo   ma · re · ni · ki · te

CHORUS.

slow

Na · dzu · to · mo   tsu · ki · nu   i · wa · wo · zo · to   Ki · ku · mo · ·

flat   *fast*

ta · ye · na · ri   a · dzu · ma · u · ta · ·   Ko   ye · so · ye · te   ka · zu

flat   *short*

ka · zu · ·   no · ·   Shoŏ · cha · ku   kin   ku · go   ko · un   no

flat

Ho · ka · ni   mi · chi · mi · chi · te · ·   Ra · ku · ji · tsu · no   ku · re · na ·

i · wa   so · me · i · ro · no · ·   ya · ma · wo   u · tsu · shi · te   mi · do · ri ·

wa   na · mi · ni   u · ki · shi · ma · ğa   Ha · ra · u   a · ra · shi · ni

265

'NOH'

faster   slow   flat

ha · na fu · ri · te . . Ge · ni yu · ki · wo me · gu · ra · su

slow

ha · ku wun · no so · de · zo ta · ye · na · ru

SHITE.

Slower   slow

Na · mu Ki · mi · o Gat · ten · shi Hon · ji Dai · sei · shi . . . .

CHORUS.

slow

a · dzu · ma · a · so · bi · no mai · no · ki · o · ku . . A · ru · i · wa

SHITE.

fast

a · ma · tsu mi · so · ra · no mi · do · ri · no ko · ro · mo

CHORUS.

Slow

Ma · ta · wa ha · ru · ta · tsu ka · su · mi · no ko · ro · mo.

SHITE.

fast

I · ro · ka · mo ta · ye · na · ri o · to · me · no mo · su · so

fast   fast

Sa · yi · wu · sa . . . sa · yi · wu · sas · sa · tsu no ha · na · wo

266

APPENDIX IV

'NOH'

THE END